Notebook Connections

Notebook Connections

Strategies for the Reader's Notebook

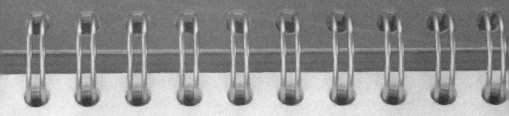

Aimee Buckner

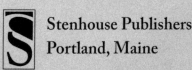

Stenhouse Publishers
Portland, Maine

Stenhouse Publishers
www.stenhouse.com

Copyright © 2009 by Aimee Buckner

Credits
Page 90: "Dreams," from *The Collected Poems of Langston Hughes* by Langston Hughes, edited by Arnold Rampersad with David Roessel, Associate Editor, copyright © 1994 by The Estate of Langston Hughes. Used by permission of Alfred A. Knopf, a division of Random House, Inc.

Library of Congress Cataloging-in-Publication Data

Buckner, Aimee E. (Aimee Elizabeth), 1970-
    Notebook connections : strategies for the reader's notebook / Aimee Buckner. p. cm.
    ISBN 978-1-57110-782-4 (alk. paper)
1. Reading comprehension. 2. Note-taking--Study and teaching (Elementary) 3. Children--Books and reading. 4. School notebooks. I. Title.
    LB1573.7B83 2009
    372.47--dc22
                                                            2009009213

Cover, interior design, and typesetting by Designboy Creative Group

Manufactured in the United States of America on acid-free, recycled paper
15 14 13 12 11 10 09   9 8 7 6 5 4 3 2 1

For the teachers and staff
at Brookwood Elementary School
(1997-2008)

Contents

Acknowledgments ix

Chapter 1: *Reading, Writing, and Harvesting Hope* 1

Chapter 2: *Invitations: Getting to Know Students as Readers*................. 13

Chapter 3: *From Comprehension Strategies to Notebooks* 37

Chapter 4: *Reading Like a Writer*... 59

Chapter 5: *Beneath the Story: Discovering Hidden Layers*...................... 87

Chapter 6: *Assessment: A Tool for Teaching in the Now* 113

Appendix...139

References 145

Strategy Lessons

Character Connections 105

Connotation 93

The Fab Five 55

Favorite Authors 78

Finding the Spark 35

History of a Reader 27

Leaning In 42

Lifting a Prompt 111

Reread to Lift a Line 48

Summarizing Questions 57

Theme 98

What I Know to Be True About Reading 20

What Keeps You Reading? 26

Writing Connections 51

Acknowledgments

Just as it takes a village to raise a child, it takes many people to write a book. First and foremost, I'd like to thank the teachers and staff at Brookwood Elementary School for their generous support of me and all of my projects. And thanks for still smiling when the little projects turn out to be big ones.

Sometimes I need a nudge to keep pushing myself not only to write but also to continue my own professional learning journey. Thank you to Karen Head, Cheri Carter, and Debbie Cherry for making professional learning an expectation and a reality at our school.

I'm blessed to work alongside teachers who inspire me to learn more and to continue to work hard even on the difficult days: Debbie Leonard, Tina Pimental, Cheryl Cole, Bobbie Williams, Pam Wallace, and Nina MacKellar. A special thank-you to Jennifer Moon for sharing your insights and practices regarding writing about what kids read.

In my own pursuit of professional learning, I find inspiration in the work of Stephanie Harvey, Anne Goudvis, Franki Sibberson, Jen Allen, Ralph Fletcher, Lola Schaefer, April Pulley Sayre, and Rebecca Dotlich. Thank you for your encouragement and words of wisdom. Whether you've helped me directly with this book or with other work, you all have influenced my writing and the way I teach my students. Brenda Power, thank you for making me a part of your Choice Literacy family and believing in me.

Thank you to the teachers who tried these lessons with their students and gave me valuable feedback: Cindy Beebe, Kathy McKinzey, Sally Hollyfield, Cheryl Cole, Cameron Franklin, Jennifer Moon, and Kimberly Watkins. And thank you to the many students who helped develop these strategies in their own effort to make sense of what they're reading.

It's difficult to find time to write. Thank you to Chris (Mom) DiMuzio and Heather Horton for all of the babysitting. Thanks (and hugs) to my son Michael for putting up with all the babysitting.

For holding my hand through this process, nudging me when needed, pushing when nudging didn't work, and always being so very nice, thanks to my editor, Philippa Stratton; this book would not be without her guidance. Chris Downey, Nancy Sheridan, and the Stenhouse team did a great job shaping my manuscript into this book. Jen Allen read and reread the manuscript—thank you for your help and response. And to Jeff Anderson, my friend and Stenhouse sibling, Brenda likes me best!

Chapter 1

Reading, Writing, and Harvesting Hope

It was the middle of the school year, and my class and I had grown quite comfortable with each other—sharing stories and ideas in reading and writing workshops. The class had come together as a community of caring students—with one or two glitches along the way. But it was the time of year that real conversations were happening about what we were reading and writing.

I had just finished reading *Harvesting Hope: The Story of Cesar Chavez* by Kathleen Krull (2003), a picture book biography of Chavez and how he led a statewide, peaceful protest in California to gain rights for migrant workers. It is a beautifully written story of his life, one that I knew was a life my middle-class, southern students would not have experienced.

The children were writing on sticky notes, collecting facts, questions, and responses from the story (Harvey 1998). I gave the children time to post their notes on a class chart before we began our conversation. The fact column went routinely without much ado. It was when we got to the questions and responses that I started to fall under the spell that teachers feel when things go way beyond the planned lesson.

Questions included the following:

How did they live without a bathroom in their hut?

How can you share a bathroom with so many people?

What kind of work did the children do?

How does a family live off of five dollars a week?

Were they hungry?

Were they scared?

Why couldn't they speak Spanish in school?

Did he know Martin Luther King, Jr.?

These questions went beyond simple comprehension. My students were trying to grapple with this story in which they had no schema to pull from. They were trying to connect their own life to the story, but the connections were lost in the gap between their life and that of Cesar Chavez.

As we discussed the possible answers to these questions, our understanding of the difference between our lifestyle and Chavez's deepened, allowing for a deeper understanding of the story as well. On further reflection, though, I realized that these were not just readers' questions, but questions of writers. We could research the answers to these questions and write a report or an information guide for the text. We could also put these questions in our writer's notebooks and allow ourselves to wonder how they might be answered, imagining how these things would look in our life today: What would it be like to share a bathroom with everyone in our family? Or, What would it be like to have my very own bathroom and not have to share with anyone?

When our discussion moved to the response column, there were "typical" student responses like, "That is sad he couldn't speak Spanish in school," or, "I wouldn't want to share the bathroom with other families." But sprinkled in these responses were thoughts that revealed deeper thinking.

* *I felt sad when the teacher hung the sign on his neck that said, "I am a clown. I speak Spanish." It was like when the teacher put the red sweater on the girl's desk in "Eleven."*

• *This story is like the article we read about children picking bananas. Is this story from today or a long time ago? Is this still happening?*

- *Cesar Chavez reminds me of Martin Luther King, Jr. He is a smart man who believes in peace, not violence. Why aren't there white people like that?*

- *I don't know what it is like to be poor. I'm lucky, I guess.*

- *This story makes me want to cry and laugh. I can't believe it is really true.*

- *This is like that article we read about the children who have to work picking bananas instead of going to school.*

These are fourth-grader responses? I couldn't believe it. I hadn't planned on this type of deeper thinking or the connections the children were making between texts. But what does a teacher do with this kind of reading comprehension? The children obviously understood the story and were synthesizing the information to create new understanding. But when they came to write, I was disappointed by their responses.

Today we read, Harvesting Hope by Kathleen Krull. It was really good. It was about a boy who was living in Mexico and had to move to the United States. Then he had to go to work picking grapes. His family didn't have a home anymore. They moved from farm to farm to work for a little money. Then he grew up and got other workers to stop working until farmers treated them fairly. He walked through all of California to the statehouse to get someone to listen to him. Cesar Chavez was a great man like Martin Luther King, Jr. I thought it was sad he couldn't speak Spanish in school. I wonder what it would be like to lose my home and have to go to work like he did.

Entries like this didn't reflect the nature or depth of the conversation we had in class. After spending a full hour on that book and related conversation, students' written responses didn't seem to capture the significance of what I thought they should have learned. And, as a teacher faced with time constraints, an overloaded curriculum, and ridiculous pass/ fail tests looming in the months ahead, I had to take stock: Was I using my class time wisely if the written responses did not capture the essence of student understanding as verbalized in the class conversation?

Deep down, I know these conversations that take place after reading beautiful texts like *Harvesting Hope* are ones that I'll refer to throughout the year. Because of the rich conversation, the book becomes an anchor text that students will revisit over and over again. But the talk didn't spill over into the students' written responses like I wanted, not yet.

So, Where Is the Hope?

As teachers, our anxiety to do well and to teach the curriculum while pretending not to be bothered by all of the testing that takes place sends hope into hiding. But when I sat down and thought about what I know is true about how children learn, I realized a few things. First, teaching students how to read and comprehend what they're reading is complicated. It's not like teaching writing, where the writing process is so similar for most writers. With reading, you have to consider fluency, comprehension strategies, word work, plot structure, literary elements, different genres, and everything that is lumped into the "skills" category. Second, students need time. They need time to read without the interruptions of sticky notes and thinkmarks. They need time to develop and fine-tune their own thinking processes while reading. They need time to talk about books and write about all that stuff that goes on in their head while reading. And third, children will not write well when they are overwhelmed or bored. If I have students writing in every subject, every day about deep, thoughtful topics that take a lot of brain power, it stands to reason that nine-year-olds will get tired and not write well from day to day. Or if I have a standard format for them to write to me about their books, the writing becomes formulaic and automatic with buzzwords to keep me thinking they're thinking when we both know they're not. I'm embarrassed at how many times I was thrilled with responses to literature because the student used the word *infer* or *visualize.* When I look back, the entries may actually resemble a traditional spelling assignment to write the words in a sentence: *I* visualized *the story. I* inferred *and I was right.*

When looking at this and at what my students need to know for "the test," it's no wonder I didn't see the hope. But it's there. Hope, that feeling that what we want to accomplish in our classrooms with our students can be done, is something I have to keep in the forefront of my mind as I plan. It keeps me looking ahead at what my students can do rather than what they're not doing. Hope, for me, is keeping focused on the goal—lifetime readers and writers—and continuing to work toward that goal, rather than worrying about the obstacles that loom ahead. Hope is immersing my students in quality literature and the many reading and comprehension strategies that they can learn to use effectively. It's giving kids time to develop their strategies for reading and comprehension and learning to use them automatically. Hope is what starts as a feeling and a belief, about my students as learners, and grows into reality. It slowly changes from a vision in my mind to experiences in my classroom as we tend to the complicated act of reading with anticipation and joy rather than dread and the threat of a looming test.

Strategies That *Do* Work

I'm a lifetime member of Weight Watchers. It's true. And, unfortunately, just because I know how to lose weight and keep it off doesn't mean I do. But when I gain weight, I think about what I know. I know the point system works for me. I know I can't eat peanut butter with every meal. I know that I need to drink water. But actually following through with all of this is a very different story. It's that way with teaching. I know a lot about how to teach writing, and I know a lot about how to teach reading. What took a while was figuring out how to connect what I know about teaching these two subjects to affect student achievement.

I know that keeping a writer's notebook as part of one's writing process helps writers think and plan their next writing project. I've seen it work with veteran and professional writers as well as with student writers. I know that relying on writing strategies to ignite thinking helps writers get started each day and yet does not get in the way of deeper thinking. In using writer's notebooks, I'd seen students go from thinkers of writing (I'm thinking every day for forty-five minutes so I don't have to write) to writers who think. The question I grappled with was how to move students from "couch-potato" readers who read words and can answer basic questions with one word to readers who think while reading, and then on to readers who think beyond their reading. When I realized that one way to do this would be to show students how strategies that help us write our own stories can also help us write about stories we read, I had found the bridge I was looking for. And in the reader's notebook I had found the place for them to document their thinking and growth, to support their thinking for group discussions, and to explore their own ideas about a text without each and every entry being a judgment of their reading progress. My students value this tool just as they value their writer's notebooks. It becomes a part of who they are in fourth grade. Meanwhile, it gives me insight as to how they are approaching text and what happens to the story once it's set free in their minds.

I had several guides pointing the way to this bridge. Stephanie Harvey and Anne Goudvis have ignited a revolution concerning explicit teaching of reading comprehension strategies—ways readers think. Although *Strategies That Work* (2000/2007) wasn't the first book out on the subject, it has been the most influential. The strategies they write about have altered how teachers and students think about reading—literally. They have made us more aware of the cognitive practices great readers do naturally and the rest of us have to practice and learn to use intentionally.

Katie Wood Ray has influenced as many teachers to read like writers. Her books, *Wondrous Words* (1999) and *Study Driven* (2006), have given teachers a backstage look at texts we love to read. She has shown us how to read like writers—finding the craft within the text and then trying it out in our own writing. In *Study Driven*, she takes it a step further with genre studies, connecting books and craft under the umbrella structure of a genre. Her work continues to inspire teachers to look more closely at the writing of language in hopes of transferring it to our own written work.

JoAnn Portalupi and Ralph Fletcher continue to give teachers resources in a quick and direct way to help them become more informed about their teaching of writing. With books and kits like *Craft Lessons* (2007) and *Teaching the Qualities of Writing* (2004), the authors have focused lessons to lift the quality of student writing while resting it on the shoulders of quality literature. With a sense that teachers don't always have the time and energy to read through complex text to figure out what to do, they provide the "teacher's editions" to writing workshop.

These resources are like pieces of a quilt—different fabrics representing different parts of a reader's and writer's life. Each piece has meaning and will fit with other pieces. Yet there needs to be someone or something to stitch it all together. We know that thread is there—connecting all of this together—we just can't see it when the quilt is finished. And isn't that how it should be? In order to get the parts to fit, something has to hold it all together. Within the context of reading and writing workshop, I have found the thread that works for me—a notebook approach.

From Hope to Reality

This book is about making your hope into a reality for your students. It's about using a reader's notebook as a tool to capture student thinking and understanding about text. Relying on what I know about teaching writing and from my experiences that brought me to write *Notebook Know-How: Strategies for the Writer's Notebook* (2005), I've developed a reader's notebook model that is flexible enough for students to respond in a variety of ways, yet structured enough to provide explicit instruction. The reader's notebook strategies in this book are set up in a similar manner to the writing strategies in my earlier book. They're meant to be teacher-guided lessons for students to create anchor texts within their notebooks. Then as children become more independent in their thinking and response, they begin to respond in their notebooks, choosing strategies that work best for them. Eventually, all of this writing could lead to literary essays or formal responses of some sort. Although I may do some of this in my classroom, the purpose of this book is to look at the reader's notebook as its own entity and to invite you to explore its possibilities in your classroom.

There is so much to say about the teaching of reading, and this is reflected in the size of some of those comprehensive, seminal books on the topic. Teachers have dubbed Fountas and Pinnell's book *Guiding Readers and Writers Grades 3–6* (2001) "the phone book" because it is so thick and packed with useful information. Lucy Calkins's *The Art of Teaching Reading* (2000) is no lightweight, nor is Harvey and Goudvis's *Strategies That Work* (2000/2007).

In writing, as in life, I favor the Weight Watchers approach. I know students need a place to explore their ideas. I know students need guidance to move their reading responses beyond "The book is good." I know strategies work and that putting all of this together is the art of teaching.

This book is based on reading theory, comprehension strategies, and trial and error. It's a book that zeros in on using a reader's notebook as a tool for students to generate and elaborate on responses to text. It's a book of strategies students can rely on—from book to book, from genre to genre—that will push their writing beyond retelling the story.

In addition, there is a section in this book that addresses the seemingly elusive connection between reading and writing. We all know it's there and, supposedly, if we read a lot and write a lot, the two will magically come together. POW! Our students become brilliant. The reading-writing connection is a bridge of understanding that helps the reader write more reflectively about his or her reading and the writer write more purposefully for his or her reader. Taking time to focus on this bridge in the reader's notebook gives students the opportunity to think both as a reader and a writer.

And, of course, this book will look at how reader's-notebook entries find their way to my grade book. There, I said it. I'm a teacher and I grade things. But, I'm still in the classroom, and I think that way. The fact is, I can't put a grade on a report card based on conversations. (However, that would be better than putting a grade on a report card based on workbook pages.) So there is a gap between the grade and a need to see student comprehension, to find evidence of thinking, and to create a history of growth as a reader. Writing about reading isn't the only way to do this; as I've said before, teaching reading is complicated. But it is one way to hold on to student thinking over the course of time.

The bottom line is, I have had to accept that comprehension isn't always tangible. It's not something I'll always be able to hold in my hand and say to a parent, "See, your child comprehends." Reading comprehension is a lifelong process—as we grow and gather different life experiences, our understanding of text changes. Louise Rosenblatt's work enables us to understand that the "literary work must hold out some link with the young reader's own past and present preoccupations, emotions, anxieties, ambitions" (2005, 65). And as long as we're living, we bring to the text a different set of values and experiences than other readers and even the author. Since this relationship between the text and the reader is unique, to trap this process in the form of a question, journal entry, or essay is difficult to say the least. Capturing this relationship in a grade is nearly impossible. Yet, for those of us required to keep grades and report progress as such, I'll examine ways to assess the notebook without totally undermining the process from which it came.

The Notebook Approach

Relying on what I know works for writer's notebooks, I have twisted, turned, and modified writing strategies to work with reading (see Figure 1.1). In the writing workshop, my students keep writer's notebooks to collect their ideas and thoughts about stories they're writing. We also look at the structure of language through grammar and usage and keep notes in these notebooks. In the reading workshop, my students keep reader's notebooks. These are notebooks in which we keep our thinking regarding other people's writing in books and articles. We also keep notes about how authors use language in interesting ways. We zero in on literary elements that authors use to develop their stories and relate how it affects us as the reader. And we develop and extend our understanding of comprehension strategies as we tackle different texts from different genres.

Figure 1.1

	Writer's Notebook	Reader's Notebook
Strategies	Strategies help writers develop ideas for writing pieces. Strategies are used throughout the writing process to support the writer in completing a finished piece.	Strategies help readers focus their thinking— giving them choices for how to respond to a text. Strategies may be used over a period of time as a reader completes a text and may be reused with a new text.
Entries	Entries are about a page long, giving the gist of a story or the writer's thinking about a topic. Writers purposefully explores a topic for writing using several entries in a row. Writers use notebook entries to try out writer's craft that may be used in a draft. Writers eventually use the entries to create finished pieces of writing outside of the notebooks.	Entries may be as short as a few sentences or as long as a page. Entries may lead to a new line of thinking with the text. They are a placeholder for ideas the reader wants to share with others or to further explore on his or her own. Patterns of thinking may appear through entries for a similar book or across texts.
Assessment	Assessment is based on a preponderance of evidence over several entries. A rubric is used to guide this holistic approach.	Assessment is based on a preponderance of evidence over several entries. A rubric is used to guide this holistic approach.

So this is the bridge. It's a bridge made of notebooks—plain old paper stuck together in some fashion—traveled heavily by thinkers. It's the bridge for readers and writers to cross, meet, and influence each other. Book by book, strategy by strategy, and page by page, the readers in my classroom are able to cross the bridge and make my hope a reality.

Chapter 2
Invitations: Getting to Know Students as Readers

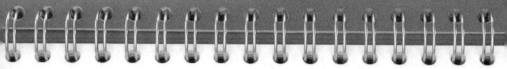

My reading file cabinet seems to get fuller as the years go by, and yet I rarely go into it to use what I have in there. This year, I decided, after moving classrooms yet again, that I should weed through the papers.

I guess it's here that I admit that I can totally relate to Templeton the rat in *Charlotte's Web*. Not that I'm inconsiderate, selfish, and grouchy all of the time, but I collect everything and throw away nothing. And if you save enough, there is bound to be a rotten egg in there somewhere that needs to be thrown out.

So I found myself in my windowless and air-conditionless classroom in the middle of a warm Georgia summer day riffling through papers stuffed in the top drawer of my file cabinet. The electric fans blowing cool air foreshadowed the oncoming onslaught of paper airplanes I was bound to make, because I realized that there was a good reason I hadn't reused a lot of my reading stuff. It was trash.

For example, I found eight different reading surveys. *Eight*. They all had similar questions but different ways to answer. Reading surveys help me get to know my students as readers. Knowing what makes my kids tick is essential to how I plan, and the reading surveys give me a quick look at some general aspects of their reading. However, I realized that if I already had eight, maybe it was not another survey I was looking for.

Although surveys may give me an introduction, there are no shortcuts to teaching reading, and to really know how to help each student, we have to know them. This is why I depend on student responses in the reader's notebook to introduce me to the reader inside them. With the reader's notebook, students have many opportunities to demonstrate the kind of reader and thinker they were before the school year, the one they are right now during the school year, and the one they will grow into as the year progresses.

Getting to know my students as readers is as important as getting to know them as writers. Taking what I know about writing and writer's notebooks, it finally dawned on me—or more likely nailed me on the head like a cartoon sledgehammer: I needed to get to know my readers through their own words. My approach needed to be child centered. Hence I've integrated the notebook format—strategies and writing time—into my reader's notebooks.

Launching Strategies

When launching the reader's notebook, it's important for students to understand that this is their notebook and these are their ideas, and that they're in control of how they respond. My job is to guide them, help them approach their thinking in ways that focus what they want to write. Strategies do that. Strategies are different from prompts in that they can be used more than once in different situations. A prompt, by nature, tends to be used for a specific purpose with a specific book. A prompt also is very directive in the kind of response that is expected—funneling student thoughts to a specific end. A strategy tends to be more open-ended—inviting readers to think about elements of books and genres in order to draw their own conclusions and respond in ways that seem natural to them.

One of the most alluring aspects of literature circles as described by Harvey Daniels (2002) are the "jobs"—approaches or lenses through which students can respond to the reading. These approaches help kids channel their thinking yet keep it open enough for them to respond in ways that seem natural and appropriate to the reader. But the downfall when giving a child a specific role or job for a specific reading is that it limits how they can respond at any particular juncture. Teachers who have learned to use literature circles effectively know that assigning the roles isn't as important as children knowing various ways they might choose to respond.

It's the same thing with reader's notebook strategies. The purpose is to give students choices and ideas of how to respond to their reading. Sometimes being too open-ended is overwhelming and being too restrictive leads to contrived responses. It's a delicate balance. I try to find that balance between the two in the strategies I use.

It's true that in the beginning of the year, children are trying to figure out what the teacher *wants*. I remember as a student going through the same anxiety. Will my best work be good enough for this teacher? Or, Can I get away without trying very hard and still make As? I see these questions dancing through some of my students' thought bubbles the first weeks of school. In addition, many of my students have not kept reader's notebooks before. Most of them have come from classrooms where they either wrote weekly literature letters, responded to specific prompts, or wrote book reports. I'm not saying any of these things in and of themselves are wrong—they're just different from the notebook.

In order to get things started, maybe for the first quarter or so, I use the strategies for guided practice. What I mean is I model the strategy with our read-aloud, and then I ask the students to try this same strategy when responding to the book they're reading independently or in guided reading. This way, they can practice the strategy with a text that is just right for them. The strategies are a bit restrictive, because I'm not giving students a choice of how to respond. But I've learned that unless children know what the choices are, they can't choose well. So the first part of the year is more guided than the rest of the year.

As children start to become more independent using the strategies, I will hand over the responsibility of choosing a strategy that seems right for them. Kids eventually respond in their notebook once or twice a week, choosing different strategies to help push their thinking about the book. I find this works well for kids who are reading with a partner, in a small group, in a literature circle, or independently. It's not one size fits all, but rather an approach that is easy to differentiate among readers and books.

Like the writer's notebook, the reader's notebook becomes a place where kids of all levels can shine. It becomes a part of who they are as a reader and slows them down just enough to honor their thinking without distracting them from their book. This notebook approach has led my speed readers—the ones who finish a book in a day or two and then move on to the next one—to begin to see the value in taking some thinking time. It has led many of them to reread books, looking for clues and ideas they might have missed earlier.

This approach has also kept my struggling readers motivated. Strange but true. By the upper grades, kids hate that they're still struggling to read. They'll do anything to fit in. This notebook approach allows readers to respond to their own book, using strategies similar to everyone else's. Lifting some of the anxiety that rests on their shoulders frees them to focus on the reading and not on the social embarrassment of the "easy" work.

What I Know Is True

School has started and I'm back in my windowless room, this time with air-conditioning. I'm surrounded by my fourth graders, reading my all-time favorite picture book, *John Henry* by Julius Lester (1994). I start every read-aloud with the same question:

"How many of you have never heard or read this book?"

Hands shoot up and I respond, "You poor souls. I'm so glad you'll hear this today."

The children giggle, roll their eyes, and someone mumbles, "She always says that."

On this day, though, after reading the book and closing it, Dean's eyes widen and he shoots his hand into the air.

"Ms. B., you're right! We were poor souls. That was the best book ever!"

"Yeah, it gave me chills," agrees Zoe.

"How did you know, Ms. B.?" asks Emma.

"Know what?" I ask.

"Know that we needed to hear that book down to our souls," Emma replies.

Before I answer her, I pinch myself because it's still early in the year and my students are already initiating this kind of conversation. Who has classes like this! Calmly and knowingly I say, "Because there are some things I know to be true about reading."

And so begins our conversation about what is true about reading to know a book down to your soul. Some students participate while others quietly listen. This alone gives me information about who is comfortable thinking and talking about their reading habits and who is not. I start to collect information on chart paper.

What I Know to Be True About Reading

» Great books are meant to be read over and over.

» Picture books aren't just for babies.

» Short chapters have benefits.

» You can depend on a favorite author.

As the kids talk about these truths, I write them down to keep track of our thinking. Then I ask the students to get their reader's notebooks out and to respond to our conversation.

"We've been talking about what we know to be true about reading. What's true for you? How does it help you as a reader? I want you to think about what your classmates have said and what you're thinking in your head. Then put your own thoughts down in your reader's notebook."

Some students make a list. Some make an annotated list, commenting on each item. Others write in paragraphs in a more stream-of-consciousness format. But all of my students are able to respond thoughtfully.

What's True for Me About Reading
by Emma, age 9

I'm hooked on fiction. I love Tamora Pierce books! I only favor her because she is one of the best authors I have ever read! She has many series and is a quick writer, so when you finish one book you don't have to wait for the next one to come out! . . . I am NOT big on non-fiction. I hate reading it. I hate too many facts that you have to read or memorize and I usually start thinking about my day and forget what I'm reading. Bookmarks are nice but always disappear. I think they're sort of overrated in fourth grade because you should know where you've stopped. I usually use them in non-fiction because like I said above I nod off. I love Tamora Pierce but sometimes I have to take a break. If I read too much of one certain author I tend to start describing things like them.

· �֍ · ✶ · ✶ ·

What's True for Me About Reading
by Drew, age 9

I love long picture books. Pictures help me visualize different things like what might happen next. Also picture books help me understand the words. Nobody knows this but I love non-fiction books. I just love the way books tell us so much instead of people telling us. Because with people, it's like blah, blah, blah, because blah, blah, blah. Poetry really interests me. I love all the rhyming words like I'm shopping for a ball in the mall. I don't really like thin books because they bore me.

· ✶ · ✶ · ✶ ·

What's True for Me About Reading
by Emaso, age 9

»   *I like to read to myself.*

»   *I like history books.*

»   *I like books that make me think.*

»   *When I read, I like it quiet.*

»   *I love non-fiction books.*

»   *I usually read a chapter a day.*

I read mostly books that people write about other people. I'm interested in Martin Luther King, Jr.

· ❋ · ❋ · ❋ ·

What's True for Me About Reading
by Zoe, age 9

»   *I never skip words that are in a book—you could skip interesting parts.*

»   *I can't read in the car (car sick).*

»   *Some baby books are still interesting to me.*

»   *When I read I go into my own world that is about the book (makes me feel inside the book).*

»   *I don't like books that they turn into shows.*

»   *I don't like it when I read aloud.*

»   *I hate it when someone questions me about the book.*

»   *To me, non-fiction books are cool if they're about things I like.*

»   *Historical fiction is interesting because it's about Civil War and of things from old times.*

»   *I LOVE scary stories!!*

When someone questions me about the book, I don't like it. When they ask me the question, it always stores into the forget file of my brain, and then I can't explain [anything]. I LOVE scary stories because they interest me in some way. When I watch scary movies with my dad, I don't get scared at all. I usually have read the book about it.

From reading these entries by my students, I have gained great insight. They come to me as readers with distinctly different styles, likes, and dislikes. They all have different approaches and secrets to their reading that may not become apparent in a reading survey. Most important, I see my students as individual readers, which causes me to teach the reader and not the book they're reading.

I would expect students to add to these entries or revisit them throughout the year. As they change and grow as readers, what they know to be true about reading should change and grow as well. It's a good strategy to use throughout the year not only for reflective purposes but also for informal progress assessments as well.

 Strategy: What I Know to Be True About Reading

Purpose: Students reflect on what they know about reading, thereby getting to know themselves and their classmates as readers.

How: Read a favorite picture book or novel. Initiate a conversation about how you choose great books to read. There are things you know to be true about reading, and they guide your choices as a reader. What do your students know to be true about reading?

Extension: Use this same strategy throughout the year to see how student thinking changes. Use the strategy to respond to reading: What I know to be true about . . . the character, the author's style, the genre, beginnings, endings, and so forth.

What Keeps Me Reading

Early in the year, like many teachers across the country, I work diligently to teach and reteach my students how to choose a just-right book. We review the parts of the book that give us information about it. We look at how to preview a book and how to tell if it's too difficult. We practice identifying authors we enjoy and the genres of books we like best. We spend this precious class time on these procedures, because as teachers who are readers, we know that unless you have a good book in your hands, you're not going to read it.

Yet, despite my best efforts, I have those drive-through readers who pick and abandon books faster than you can order a hamburger. "As students begin to encounter more complex texts, meaning may break down beyond the word level" (Sibberson and Szymusiak 2003, 52). So often, when I ask students why they have quit their book, they respond that it's boring. It's boring because they can read it but they don't understand it. Sibberson and Szymusiak paraphrase Cris Tovani's reasons why upper-grade students may get stuck and end up abandoning books.

» *They lose track of the characters as they come up again in the story.*

» *They get confused by the format or structure of the text.*

» *They fail to recognize when the setting or narrator has changed.* (2003, 52)

These are mini-lessons and topics for guided reading groups. It's going to take time to teach students about these things to help them read more complex books, but it's driving me nuts as I notice some students changing books every day. They're either choosing books that are too easy but comfortable because they're not hard to figure out, or they're choosing books that are too difficult for them and therefore seem boring.

Learning how to choose a just-right book takes more know-how than checking to see if a child can pronounce the words on a page. It's about finding a perfect fit between the book and the reader, so the reader remains engaged in the story. This is what leads students to develop a habit of finishing books they select rather than reading a little and then finding a new title.

During the first week of school, I sat down with Denise, a student who had a reputation for abandoning books. A reputation, I might add, that she was proud to have. On Meet the Teacher Day, she introduced herself and told me, "I've made it through third grade without finishing a book. I bet I won't read one in fourth either." If that's not a challenge, I don't know what is. It was like she was daring me to try to make her read. I simply said, "I didn't read an entire book until I was twenty-one. I know all the tricks of the trade. And I think it's the saddest part of my life having missed out on books for so long. I hope that doesn't happen to you."

It wasn't quite how I had envisioned Meet the Teacher Day, and somehow I don't think my response was what Denise had wanted. But it's true; it was twenty-one years before I found the joy of reading that the rest of my family had been a part of for so long. I was a master of deception for "finishing" books, and no one seemed to know what to do about it. Although I knew Denise had met her match with me, I also knew it would take me time to teach her the skills to carry her through a book. I needed to enlist the help of the other students who knew finishing a book was cool.

Gathered around me, my students had their books and notebooks in hand. "Boys and girls, I noticed that most of you are reading the same book as yesterday."

"Well, it takes awhile to read a good book, Ms. B.," replied Dean.

"Absolutely. I'm glad none of you have abandoned or stopped reading your books yet," I replied.

"Good, because mine is over 300 pages. I'm reading the first Harry Potter book, and it's going to take awhile," said Drew.

"I want all of you to take as much time as you need to finish books you start. I'm impressed that you're not abandoning books. I'm wondering what keeps you reading the book you're reading."

There are times that fourth graders don't want to be rude, but their facial expressions led me to believe they were thinking I was a bit simpleminded. Patiently they started to explain:

"Ms. B., I have read all of the Magic Tree House Books. If she comes out with more, I'll read those too," volunteered Charlie.

"I like books with short chapters. If the chapters are too long, I lose track of what's going on," said Rachel.

"Rachel has a point. James Patterson, who writes for adults, has figured out the same thing. He writes short chapters, and I like that," I affirmed.

"In some books, I forget where I am and think I'm there. That keeps me reading when things get dull," said Zoe.

"I can relate to that. One of my favorite novels, *The Last of the Really Great Whangdoodles* by Julie Andrews Edwards, is boring at the beginning. But, after the first fifty pages, it's so good I can't put it down," I said.

"I usually give a book eighty pages before I decide to abandon a book. Sometimes an author needs to warm up," Trey added.

"Okay, it seems like we're all thinking about how and why we keep reading a book until it's finished. Take a moment to jot down your ideas in your reader's notebook."

What Keeps Me Reading
by Shyam, age 9

What keeps me reading are snake books. I like them because I can learn more about them. I like them because when I went to the Atlanta Zoo, I saw the big anaconda. That's how I started loving them.

• ❋ • ❋ • ❋ •

What Keeps Me Reading
by Emma, age 9

I'm not sure what keeps me reading. It might be the excitement and the problems. It might just be that I have to read for 20 minutes every night. It might be that the fact of watching tv and playing too much video games scares me into reading boring books. Or it could be the main idea, and it could be the back of the book, because I always read the backs or flaps about books. I'm not really sure what keeps me reading. It could be I just love to read or it could be all of the above.

· ✷ · ✷ · ✷ ·

What Keeps Me Reading
by Garrett, age 9

What keeps me reading usually is the story, because I always read the back. Sometimes I read a book's first couple of pages and see if I like it so far. If I know the author, I'll keep reading because I trust him. Sometimes if someone recommends the book, I might read it. I abandon a book if it is really boring after the first 80 pages or so. If I really like a setting or the characters, I will read the book.

· ✷ · ✷ · ✷ ·

What Keeps Me Reading
by Shiv, age 9

What keeps me reading . . . I read the table of contents to see if there might be any interesting chapters I might want to read. If 5 or more chapters are interesting, I will choose that book to read. Another way is how many pages. Why? Well, because if it is a good book, I don't want it to be too long like seven-hundred pages long. I would like it to be one-hundred to two hundred. What keeps me reading is what type of book it is. If it is a mystery, adventure, scary or action book, I'll like it.

· ✷ · ✷ · ✷ ·

What Keeps Me Reading
by Zach, age 9

What keeps me reading is when in the middle something happens and I want to keep going to see what happens. If the first few pages are good, I keep reading. If the middle starts to get boring, then I sometimes keep reading to see if it gets better. If the beginning is good, I keep reading. If the middle is boring and good, I read a little bit more and then decide. If it's good, then I definitely keep reading. If the book has really short chapters, I keep reading. If I like the characters, I keep reading. If someone recommends it to me, then I'll read it. If I like the author, I keep reading.

What Keeps Me Reading
by Zoe, age 9

» *When someone recommends a book*
» *The history of the book*
» *Word choices*
» *The way the words are written*
» *Long chapters*
» *No chapters*
» *Trust the author*
» *Read the back*
» *Characters that interest me*

Just from this kind of entry, I've learned a lot about what my students already know. They know to pick books about things they love. They know to read books by authors they like. They know that sometimes a book may seem boring, but they read on because it usually gets better. They choose books that seem manageable in page number and chapter length. They know the characters matter.

It's the beginning of the year and they're talking about choosing the right book. Using this same kind of strategy to revisit what keeps them reading later in the year, the responses are likely to evolve to connect more to the reading strategies they're learning to use.

 Strategy: What Keeps You Reading?

Purpose: To identify personal reasons why a student reads and what motivates them to finish a book.

How: Recognize students for taking more than a day to read a book. Talk about how a book might last you several days or even a week as you read a little each night. Ask the students what keeps them reading a book instead of abandoning it. Keep track of initial ideas on chart paper before sending students off to write.

Extension: Revisit this midyear and toward the end of the year to see how students evolve in their approach to finishing books. Read about why authors read—many authors have websites with that kind of information. Students can find out why their favorite authors read and what keeps them motivated during a long book.

History of a Reader

My history as a reader has affected how I teach reading to my students. I learned to read quite easily and was in the advanced group through my school career. In second grade, I went to the third-grade class to read. In junior high, I participated in a science fiction reading group for strong readers. My parents took us to the library and bookstores regularly. I looked and acted like a reader.

I never chose to read when I could do something else. I rarely remember finishing books by my own choice unless my mother read them to me or I had to for a school assignment. I loved getting new books for Christmas, but rarely finished them. On long car trips during the summer, we listened to my mom read or to books on tape. Despite being surrounded by stories, I didn't bite.

When I received my student-teaching assignment, my cooperating teacher gave me the titles of two professional books to read and told me to brush up on my children's literature during the summer prior to starting. When I arrived in the fall, not having read, I found her classroom filled with books. And it was during that time that I started reading, really reading.

I called my mom and told her that if only Beverly Cleary had written when I was a kid, I might have enjoyed reading. When I returned home that Christmas, she pulled boxes of books out of the attic. All of the books she had bought for me over the years, all of the books I had refused to read—including Beverly Cleary. Well, at least I had a start to my first class library. And it was then that I vowed to help each of my students discover the joy of finishing books.

Now I read constantly. There are stacks of books in every room of my house. Everywhere you go, there is something to read. It gets a bit messy, but it's part of who I am now. And that's why history matters. It matters where my students are in their reading lives. It matters that they become committed to reading so when they leave elementary school, they have the habit.

Strategy: History of a Reader

Purpose: For students to see their growth as readers and to acknowledge their reading habits or lack thereof. In order to see growth and to evolve as readers, it's helpful for students to know where they've started. It's also helpful to establish and convince kids that they are readers and can finish books.

How: Read *Reading Grows* by Ellen Senisi (1999). Discuss how reading changes as you change. Describe your history as a reader to your class. Talk about your current reading habits and bring in samples of what you read. Invite children to think about their history and current habits. Have them write about them in their notebooks and/or share them with a partner.

Extension: This is a strategy that should be revisited throughout the year to get the most out of it. At midyear, have students reread this entry and add to it in a different color pen or pencil. This time, however, they should note changes in themselves as readers. By the end of the year, students can reread these entries and reflect on their growth. In this way, the strategy turns into a form of self-assessment and helps students anchor their roles as lifelong readers.

Thinking About Reading

Most of my students who have attended my school for at least a year know about the comprehension strategies. They *should* know that readers think while they read. The whole act of enjoying the story is indeed a form of thinking. (My son was *shocked* to find that out!) Nonetheless, children are smart and ruthless with answers that seem complete but lack significance.

My students were reading their self-selected books as I moved around the room to confer with them. It turns out that I often lift strategies from the conversations, because kids are thinking in interesting ways and don't even realize it. This particular conference didn't expose interesting thinking, per se, but rather an interesting question readers should begin to ask themselves.

"Hi, David. Will you please find a good stopping place so we can talk?" I say. (I hate interrupting students when they read, so I'll wait a moment for them to get to a place where it's appropriate to stop.)

David stops and looks up.

"How is your book?" I ask.

"Good," he replies.

"Can you tell me a bit about the story and some of your thinking about it?"

"Well, it's about this kid, I forget his name, who wants a dog. His parents won't let him have the dog, so he hides it. I'm thinking about the story when I read it."

Freeze the conference for a moment. Two things are glaring out at me. First, he doesn't remember the name of the main character. My guess is most teachers reading this book not only know the name of the character but the title and author too. This tells me he's not paying attention to important details. The name of the main character is always important. Second, what does thinking about the story mean? What does it look like, feel like, and sound like to him? I also found it interesting that he said, "I'm thinking about the story *when* I read it." When? What about when he's not reading it? Does he think about the story then? What does he think about? And before I know it, a strategy is born. (I'll try it out on David first and see how it works.)

"David, you have a good sense of the story. Remembering the character's name is important, though. I want you to figure that out by tomorrow, and we'll talk about him. But, I'm curious about your statement that you think about the story when you read it."

"You are?" He seems genuinely surprised. I think he was hoping to get a nod and a keep-reading pat on the back and then see me move on to the next kid.

"I am. What is it that you think about when you read the story?"

"Umm. Well, I think about the words—like what they are," he starts.

I nod, waiting for him to go on.

"And, I think about what he's doing."

"What do you mean—what he's doing?" I ask.

"Well, I'm thinking that hiding the dog is cheating or something. His parents don't want the dog there," he says.

"Okay. Do you think what he's doing is wrong?" I ask him.

David shrugs.

"David, I want you to try something in your notebook today. I want you to take some time and just write about the things you're thinking about while you read. Sometimes when I do that, it helps me to sort out what I think. Then when I read some more, I have a better grasp of the story and I'm more interested in the book."

"Okay," David says. He isn't thrilled but he is willing to try.

Shiloh

I'm thinking about the words. Sometimes I know what they say, but I have to think about what they mean. I saw the movie, so I see the movie in my head. The movie went faster than the book. It's easier to watch the movie.

I think about the boy hiding the dog. His parents might get mad and let the dog go. He shouldn't trick his parents. His parents will find out. Parents always do.

I've given this informal strategy to my other students as well. I ask them to try writing about their thinking while they read the book. Many children are more sophisticated in their responses, employing the correct terms of the comprehension strategies they're using. Likewise, some kids just use the strategies like buzzwords, and their entries are much less genuine than David's.

A twist I've started to give this strategy is for kids to write about their thinking when they're not reading a book. How many times has that happened to you: you're in the car or at a meeting and you start thinking about a book you're reading. It happens to kids too. In the beginning of the year, I'll use this strategy to find out what kind of books kids have thought about outside of school. It also gives me insight as to the kind of awareness they have—or don't have—about their thinking.

This strategy—to literally write about their thinking with no strings attached—develops over time as kids become better readers and thinkers. As they learn more ways to think about a book, elements of literature, and different writing techniques, their thinking will swell through their notebook. In truth, using this strategy independently is the goal of most of the other strategies—to help children not only to be aware of their thinking but to use their thinking to become more critical readers.

Sticky Notes and Thinkmarks

It's no secret that I love school supplies. What teacher doesn't? I find school supply lists fascinating—so much so that I've started reading all of the supply lists from other schools, now that local stores keep these lists stocked for shoppers. What I've noticed over the years is that even in the age of technology when paper use is supposed to lessen, the school supply list is getting longer. This year sticky notes and highlighters caught my eye. They were on both middle school and upper elementary lists. That didn't surprise me. It did surprise me to find them on my son's second-grade school supply list as well as first-grade lists. Everyone is using them.

Knowing Anne Goudvis and Stephanie Harvey, I'm sure they had no idea the sticky-note craze they would ignite with *Strategies That Work*. (Okay, so maybe the sticky-note marketing department has had something to do with it too.) They were just trying to find a way to help kids record their thinking in a fast and convenient way when writing—or highlighting—in a book was not an option. But now, classrooms everywhere are stocked with sticky notes in different colors, sizes, and shapes.

Teachers and students use the sticky notes in a variety of ways. My students have been using them long enough in school that we were able to brainstorm a list of why readers use sticky notes.

To keep track of questions.

To mark spots we're having trouble with.

To mark favorite parts.

To write connections.

To draw a quick sketch that helps us think through the chapter.

To write a word we want to look up later.

To mark an answer to a question we had earlier.

To keep track of clues for bigger questions.

To write down thoughts as they come to us while we read.

To remind ourselves of stuff—like to recommend this book to someone.

So my students use sticky notes in a variety of ways. Sometimes I ask them to do something specific when we're all working together on the same text. Sometimes they use sticky notes for their own reasons. But time and time again, I have students with books that are plastered with sticky notes. I want to know what teachers do with all of these!

I thought about wallpapering my classroom with sticky notes. It should only take a year or two. Wouldn't that be cool to have the words of children everywhere in your room like that? And if you want to replace them, just peel them off. Goodness knows, there are more sticky notes to take their place. Unfortunately, the fire marshal down in Georgia did not take kindly to my idea. Something about a fire hazard. He actually suggested that I follow the example of his child's teacher. She uses thinkmarks—bookmarks with boxes to track thinking while kids read. (Little did he know that I have read and studied Fountas and Pinnell's work, *Guiding Readers and Writers Grades 3–6*, 2001.) I asked him what I would do with the bookmarks after the kids finished the book. They don't stick to the wall, you know. He shrugged and pointed to the recycling box as he walked out the door.

I asked Stephanie Harvey what to do with these sticky notes, and she said to put them in their reader's notebooks. Brilliant—much better than the recycling box. We started putting them in the notebooks. Now what? I'm a step-by-step kind of girl. Things that are obvious to some people are not to me. I started to think about the point I was surely missing.

What's the point of the sticky notes and the thinkmarks? Obviously, to remind readers of what they were thinking while they were reading. They're a placeholder, so students can go back and revisit their thinking, much like what I do for book groups.

When I meet with my book group, we talk about the thinking we did as we read. Some women keep notebooks; some write on the pages of the book. All we need is a little reminder to bring us back to what we were thinking at the time. Sticky notes provide that for children, but the children don't always know to use them in that way.

My son is in second grade. He reads every night and has the assignment to keep sticky notes to track his thinking. His goal for the next day is to have more sticky notes than Elizabeth, another child in his class. So we stop after each page and talk about his thinking. Then he writes his thoughts on a sticky note and plasters his pages. When we're done reading, he's more interested in counting the number of notes than he is in having read a good book. I know this is developmental, and he'll figure it out as he grows older. But it panics me—have I figured it out as a teacher of older students? Because my kids don't try to compete for the most number of sticky notes; they compete for the least amount of sticky notes that will actually complete the assignment . . . barely.

In sifting through all of this information on sticky notes, and taking into consideration my concerns and what the ultimate goal of the notes might be, I've created a strategy. It may be one others have figured out, but for those teachers like me—the step-by-step learners—here it is: Finding the Spark. Some notes will no longer make sense to the children, some will seem trite and just take up space, but some will spark a fire in their thinking. These are the ones we want to save in our notebooks.

So, each week, students take time to reread the sticky notes that are in their reading books. They revisit their thinking and reflect on what they have read and written, either in class or for homework. The ones that do not make sense to them anymore, they throw out. (Or they rip off the sticky part and recycle the paper part.) The ones that seem trite—"this is funny" or "wow!"—and do not lead to deeper thinking, they throw out. Notes that seem to connect only to their life but do not deepen their thinking about the book, they put in their writer's notebook—"My grandma visited me too." But the notes that spark deeper thinking about the book, the notes with questions that burn in the reader's mind or uncover clues to develop theories about the book, these they keep.

Generally students select one or two sticky notes that reflect this deeper thinking. From here, they put them in their reader's notebook and write about their thinking connected with that note. What's amazing about this strategy is that kids start writing fewer notes just to have notes and more notes to think more deeply. It's hard at first, so I wait to introduce this strategy until we are knee-deep in sticky notes or thinkmarks. Then, when there is something to sift through, we do.

Here are a few of Summer's sticky notes from *Night of the Twisters* (Ruckman 1986). She chooses the third one to keep and think about in her notebook response that follows.

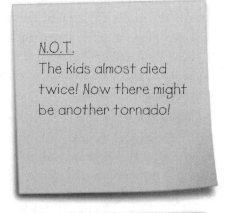

N.O.T.
This book is filled with
sad things.

* Deeper thinking below:

Summer's Response

I think there has to be a happy ending, because right now it isn't so happy and there has got to be a solution! Right now I'm worried about Dan's dad and grandparents and if there is going to be a tornado anywhere else. I would be scared if everything in my neighborhood was gone. No more pool, no more swings, no more graves, no more creek and no more forts! It would be sad to know that my whole life was just ripped to shreds—all my memories of riding bikes, berry wars, water balloon fights and kickball . . . all gone.

 Strategy: Finding the Spark

Purpose: Students keep track of their thinking as they read with sticky notes or thinkmarks. These notes accumulate quickly as a student reads a novel. This strategy gives them the time and the means to sift through their thinking and find the one or two notes that spark deeper insight into their reading comprehension.

How: After students have been tracking their thinking, ask them to reread their notes. They should make three piles: (1) the notes that do not make sense to them or just seem blah, (2) the notes that may have questions or ideas that they need to save for later in the book, and (3) those that spark their thinking right now. Pile 1 is thrown away or recycled. Pile 2 is kept and the notes are replaced in the book for further consideration. And the notes in pile 3 are transferred into the reader's notebook. Students then choose a note to write about.

Extension: After several weeks of this or after completing a novel, have the students go back and reread the notes that they have saved. Is there a pattern to their thinking? Does a theme emerge? Has the kind of things they've written down on sticky notes changed as they have learned to sift through their thinking?

With these strategies on my list, I start my school year. The interesting thing I've found is that when kids reuse the strategies—like What I Know About Reading—the list changes and grows as the kids change and grow as readers. More important, these strategies establish the notebook as a place where each student's thinking and each student's growth is evident. The strategies help me put the responsibility of thinking and writing on the students and not so much on myself. And from a practical standpoint, the notebook gives me examples to support my assessment and grades for each child. This kind of work lends credibility to the information I give parents at conference time. When I talk to them about what their child says or does in a whole-group, small-group, or individual conference conversation, the student's writing backs me up and gives the parents something to hold on to. The notebook and the writing within is the thread—connecting the conversations to individual students to parent awareness—that begins to pull the many components of reading in the upper grades together.

Chapter 3
From Comprehension Strategies to Notebooks

Our school has been studying the use of comprehension strategies for the past several years. As a staff, we have collected lessons, books, novel units, activities, websites, rubrics, and files of information on the different strategies good readers use. Now my students come to fourth grade knowing the lingo—*visualize, summarize, connect, question, determine importance,* and *synthesize.* And truthfully, I sometimes wonder what's left for me to teach.

Over the years, as I read through reader's notebooks, I was excited about students using strategy-like language until I realized that their understanding of each strategy wasn't getting deeper as they became better readers. Many still weren't aware that they were using these strategies when they read without a teacher present. Some kids didn't ask themselves questions if they weren't directed to—*that's school reading,* as one student pointed out to me. And this is the battle we all fight, isn't it? To teach children to think independently and deeply about what they read in and out of the classroom while still configuring some sort of work to fulfill the educational norms expected of a school system.

I, for one, have been guilty of teaching a whole-group lesson on a comprehension strategy and then expecting everyone to respond in their notebook on just that strategy. This isn't a bad way to introduce and begin work on a new strategy, but that's how I taught it the whole year. When I realized I was doing this—basically directing how students would think about their reading—I began to tell them to choose a strategy to focus on as they read. Well, everyone visualized. We had picture responses and only pictures. It's like the first time I tell the literature circle groups to respond to their reading with any of the "jobs" that fit their thinking. Everyone is either the illustrator or the discussion director. Hands down. So again, I'm left feeling exasperated. Why can't kids think with the maturity of an adult! Well, because they're kids.

I went back to my roots—to what I know is true about teaching. Vygotsky (1978) never fails me with his theory to teach just a little bit beyond where the students already think independently, in his zone of proximal development, that "distance between the actual developmental level as determined by individual problem-solving and the level of potential development as determined through problem-solving under adult guidance of or in collaboration with more capable peers" (Vygotsky 1978, 86). How do I get kids from the basics of the comprehension strategies to writing like the kids whose work is published in the books I've read? Again, there seemed to be a missing step for a teacher like me.

I began to realize that there are levels of thinking within some of the strategies—levels that students can identify with and use their notebooks to stretch their thinking in that direction. Discovering this for myself led me to individualizing the strategies and the reader's notebook for the different levels of students I teach. Breaking up the strategies seemed to give my stronger readers a place to go and my weaker readers a place to grow. Overall, it helped open up the notebook writing to show me the truly different kinds of thinking my students were using.

Visualizing

"Visualizing brings joy to reading" (Harvey and Goudvis 2007, 132). Isn't that the truth? When I find students who don't like to read, the very first thing I do is ask about the pictures they see in their mind. Many times a child will look at me with a blank look as if to say, I'm supposed to see things? Others will describe basic figures—"I see the character." Or, "I see a dog." As students move from picture books and chapter books with pictures to chapter books without pictures, an important text structure is missing for them. Strong readers have to provide that structure within their own mind in order to enjoy what they read.

The three levels of visualization that my classes and I have identified include still pictures, movies, and experience. In order to help students differentiate between these levels in their writing, I've tweaked the general visualizing strategy—sketching a picture—to indicate how students are "seeing" their books.

Visualizing Strategy I: Still Pictures

When readers see still pictures in their minds, the story comes across like a photo album. Each picture is separate from another picture—one picture per page of text. They visualize the story page by page, picture by picture. Many times readers will develop these pictures using the information from the book. *In the notebook*: Draw a picture and write about it.

Visualizing Strategy II: At the Movies

When readers begin to link the pictures and the character starts to move through their mind, the book unfolds like a movie. Readers actually move from reading each word and trying to make pictures, to the act of watching the book in their mind. *In the notebook:* Draw a sketch of the scenes you see playing out in your mind. Write about the things you see happening that are not in the story—the extra details your mind puts in to make the movie seem real.

Visualizing Strategy III: Experience the Story

This is the ultimate level of visualizing—actually feeling like you, the reader, have experienced the story along with the characters. You're there in the fictional world and become a part of the story. *In the notebook:* Write about your thoughts, feelings—emotional and physical—and opinions regarding the story, problem, characters, and so forth. Pay attention to details that anchor you to this world when you read. When you're not reading, what things in the story does your mind drift back to? What is the afterthought?

· ✳ · ✳ · ✳ ·

Layering this strategy for my students in different levels has opened up their eyes to the different ways readers might visualize. No longer is this a cute picture activity for my students. Many of my better readers were thinking that visualizing was a baby strategy—only beginners need to do it when they begin reading chapter books. Understanding that visualizing is more than seeing a picture in your head has helped my students push their thinking in regards to how they visualize. It also helps them monitor their thinking. If they are used to seeing movies and suddenly they find themselves in a book where they can only make a still picture, the book is taking more concentration for them. It may be that the content or words are more difficult. Students don't have to abandon the book, but they can acknowledge that they are moving to more challenging text and need to refocus their concentration rather than trying to zip through it. Likewise, the first time a child really experiences a book, it's like no other. The surprised look on a child's face when she or he first discovers that magical world and finally knows what it's like to be *in* a story makes the struggle of teaching and learning worth it. It makes me feel like I've saved a child's reading life. A bit dramatic, but true. It's hard to really experience a book and then not continue to read the rest of your life.

Leaning In

Picturing the story is something children learn from the very beginning as readers. Through wordless picture books to easy readers all the way to novels, picturing the story becomes a natural part of reading. So when kids go to work in their reading notebooks, they often take for granted that everyone sees a similar picture or movie. What is normal for them in their mind's eye may be wondrous to another reader.

A notebook strategy I teach my students is to lean in and look at their pictures in ways others may not. This strategy can be used with all the levels of visualization, so all children can work within their notebooks at their own ability.

While reading *The Fairy-Tale Detectives* (2007) from the series The Sisters Grimm by Michael Buckley, I paused after the characters were reunited with their grandmother. "When I picture this in my mind, I can see the girls and the grandmother hugging, just like the author says in the story." Children agreed that they saw that in their minds too. I continued, "Does anyone notice how Sabrina is hugging her grandmother?"

"What do you mean?" asked Drew.

"How does Sabrina look in your mind while she's hugging her grandmother at the end of the book?" I explained.

"Well, she's hugging her—you know, with her arms wrapped around her waist," Drew responded.

"I see her really squeezing her grandmother, like she has finally accepted her," said Emma.

"Yeah, not like in the beginning of the story when the grandmother hugged Sabrina. Sabrina didn't hug back. This time she hugs back; she believes it's her grandmother," said Drew.

"When I think about this scene and lean in for a closer look, I see Sabrina hugging with both hands and squeezing really tight too. I think I also see her hands gripping her grandmother's shirt, like she doesn't want to let go. I'm thinking this is Sabrina's way of holding on to her family," I added. "Sometimes when I can picture a scene in my mind and it seems important but I don't really know why, then I try to lean in and see what details I may be missing. Like Sabrina's grip on her grandmother."

Student Sample: Garret

Harry Potter and the Sorcerer's Stone by J. K. Rowling

"Mr. Ollivander had come so close that he and Harry were almost nose to nose."

I picture them really close to each other. Their noses almost touch and they're looking into each other's eyes. I imagine Mr. Ollivander is like a hunchback, so his neck swoops down a little, making him Harry's height. Harry's face looks a little surprised and scared at the same time. Mr. Ollivander's face looks like he's looking for something in Harry's eyes.

 **Strategy:** Leaning In

Purpose: Leaning In is a strategy to help students see (infer) details that may be in their mind but the author didn't necessarily write. This helps students infer why these details matter and derive meaning from the text.

How: During a read-aloud, stop at a point to discuss the picture in your mind. In the example above, I used *The Fairy-Tale Detectives*, one of the books in Michael Buckley's series, The Sisters Grimm. Lead the discussion to model how you lean in to see more of the scene. It's like pausing a movie to look at one frame or taking a magnifying glass to a picture. Discuss (or write about) the details and the meaning you infer from them.

Writing Connection: When students write their own stories, they should consider the details they use for the reader. When trying to teach students to "show don't tell," the Leaning-In strategy can also work. Students find a place in their writing that they can see in their mind. Then, they lean in and look for the details in their mind that they didn't write. From there they can add the details to help their readers see a similar picture.

Digging In: Helping Children Gain a Deeper Understanding of Text

In writing, I often have kids look at a particular excerpt from a published work to focus their attention on the writing of the text. It's like we step aside from the writing we're working on for a moment to look more carefully at a piece of writing we admire. We circle words we like, underline phrases we love, and notice as much as we can about how this part was put together. Once students see how an author crafts his or her writing, they are more likely to imitate those techniques in their own work.

In reading, I use small, guided reading groups as opportunities for children to reread an excerpt together. In doing so, I'm able to help support *and deepen* their understanding of the books and articles we read. As we do in writing, I have my students reread the text I've chosen to focus on that day. The children highlight clues, words, or sentences that help them better understand the text as well as practice the notebook strategy we're using in class. It's a great way to support struggling readers who are overwhelmed with the idea of reading a whole book, writing sticky notes for all of these strategies, and thinking deeply to write entries in their notebook. The guided reading group becomes a gulp of air for kids drowning in the amount of reading and thinking we do in class. But it's also a time for me to pull students out to form groups and show them how to use strategies to dig deeper into the texts we're reading.

Guided Reading Group with Alon, Madison, Roasia, and Hannah

Aimee: From talking with you in your reading conferences and reading your notebooks, I think we need to work on drawing conclusions together.

Alon: *Yes*! I have no idea what that means.

Roasia: Me neither.

Aimee: Okay, well it's a terrible-sounding phrase that means to infer—to use details from the story and your own thinking to figure out what is going on in the story. It's like putting together pieces of a puzzle to see the whole picture.

Hannah [*with a look that says go on . . .*]: Okay?

Aimee: For example, if I told you I was going to my mom's house for dinner tonight and was bringing a present and a cake, what could you say about that? Draw a conclusion—infer.

Madison: I know. It's a birthday party.

Roasia: Is it your mom's birthday? You wouldn't bring your own present.

Aimee: You're both right. It's a birthday party for my mom's birthday. Roasia, you used something I told you—a clue. You said I brought a present. What else clued you in to the idea it was a birthday party and not Christmas or another holiday?

Alon: The cake!

Aimee: You got it! Now we're going to look at an excerpt from *Goblins in the Castle* by Bruce Coville. It's a part we've already read about the character Igor. As you reread this section, I want you to highlight details or clues that the author gives us to help us know the character better.

[*After the girls have time to work, the discussion continues.*]

Aimee: What did you notice?

Hannah: He said nobody bops Igor.

Aimee: Okay, and what do you think that says about Igor?

Hannah: People are afraid of him?

Aimee: Yes. What else did you notice?

Alon: I highlighted, "Igor like William. Igor let William hold bear." I think that means Igor trusts William but that's unusual. Igor doesn't have many friends.

Aimee: What makes you say he doesn't have many friends?

Madison: It's not in this part, it's earlier in the book.

Aimee: You're getting the hang of this. Authors often leave clues in the details, and as readers, we sometimes skip over the details when we read. So I want you to be careful of that. Go ahead and glue this excerpt into your reader's notebook. I'd like you to write an entry using what you learned today in our group.

Roasia: Does it have to be based on this?

Aimee: Today it does, so that you remember what we did. Tomorrow we'll work on reading and writing the details on sticky notes or thinkmarks instead of working on the text.

Roasia: Igor doesn't have any friends. He's in the dungeon. I think he uses his bear as a weapon to hit others. Maybe Igor is a guard in the dungeon and he is afraid of the prisoners. I think it's sad that Igor is all alone. William is like Igor. He doesn't have any friends either. I think that's sad too. I have lots of friends. I'd be sad without them. Maybe William and Igor will become BFF [Best Friends Forever]!

Lifting a Line

Rereading in writing is essential, but it's often seen as a waste of time in reading class. Before each read-aloud I ask my students who has never read this book, and there are kids who call out, "I read that last year!" To them I say, "You are so lucky. You get to reread and discover all of the clues and moments you missed the first time you read this." Amazingly enough, they do.

In his book *Deeper Reading*, Kelly Gallagher (2004) talks about the need for students to experience multiple readings of texts. "Much like 'reading' a complex film, reading a complex book requires the reader to revisit it if a deeper appreciation is to be developed" (80). He refers to the initial reading as "first-draft reading" and says that "students come to us with an 'I read it—I'm done' mentality. It is up to us to show them the value of second-draft reading" (80). It is in these subsequent readings that they can find the details, clues, symbolism, and so on.

It's October and I'm reading *Goblins in the Castle* by Bruce Coville (1992). It's one of my all-time favorites, and I've read it year after year after year to my third, fourth, and fifth graders. Since most of them have not heard the book before, I had them engage in several readings of the book. First, I had students preread chapters independently before we read them together. This allowed me time to use this assignment with a guided reading group. Then we would read the chapters together, out loud. This helped students to fill in some of the gaps that they missed when they read independently. For homework, I had them reread the chapters. On this third read, students were looking for clues and ideas they might have missed earlier. I had kids fake it and say they did the reading when I knew they didn't. But the more the other children found interesting things they had missed, the more buy-in I got from the rest of the class. Soon there was no doubt in my mind that students were reading the chapters more than once.

"Boys and girls, we have been talking about the details or moments we miss the first time we read a chapter or book. When I'm rereading at home, it's helpful for me to write in my reader's notebook about the things I want to share with you the next day. One way I do this is when I find a part that I had read the first time but only really paid attention to the second time I read it, I lift that line. For example, when William and Igor left the castle, William noticed how bright it was outside and that the mist was gone from around the tower. I have read that part many times, but this time, I noticed the mist was gone and so were the goblins. The outside was bright and sunny when earlier in the story it was dark and rainy. I'm thinking the author is trying to send me a message—like there is a connection between the mist and the goblins, the bad weather with the goblins' capture, and the good weather with the goblins' release. It makes me wonder if the goblins were bad and brought bad weather to the castle or if they were good and the bad weather was caused by the evil spell keeping them there.

"As I think about this, I want to write it down in my notebook. First I write the line from the book that sparked my thinking. When I rewrite the line exactly, I'll put it in quotes and write the page number. This is lifting a line—I'm taking a line right out of the book so I can write about it. Beneath this, I'll write my thinking about this part and how it has me thinking about the book."

With third and fourth graders, I use a gradual release of responsibility model (Pearson and Gallagher 1983). We'll look for a line together while we read a chapter. Then we'll talk about it and write about it in our notebooks. Kids will later work in pairs doing something similar, and, eventually, students will start to use this strategy on their own.

Student Sample: Zoe

Mr. Tucket by Gary Paulsen

"He had the scalps of many 'victories' braided around the doorway to his lodge."

What I'm wondering about this sentence right now is what the heck does this mean!!? I honestly think that it means that Braid had scalps from dead people's heads braided around his doorway. But how do you braid scalps? That's what I want to know! If all I just said is true, then it probably means that either Braid is a murderer or he just likes souvenirs from his victims or both!

Student Sample: Huldana

Poppy by Avi

"Let's just hope your presence will convince him that, one, you truly are apologetic for what you have done, and two, in the future, you will ask for his permission before venturing anywhere."

What I think is interesting about this sentence is Poppy's father, Lungwort, would really let Poppy go with him to see Mr. Ocax.

Doesn't Lungwort know that Poppy may be eaten by Mr. Ocax?! It is like my father taking me to a murderer's house and hoping he doesn't kill me. Doesn't Lungwort care if Poppy lives or dies? She's his daughter! Maybe Poppy will be a sacrifice for Mr. Ocax so the rest of the mice can live.

 Strategy: Reread to Lift a Line

Purpose: Students learn that rereading is a helpful technique to use to understand text. Often kids see rereading as a weakness, but when put in the context of "second-draft reading," it becomes an expectation. Good readers miss details and so they reread. Having the story already in mind frees readers to pay attention to things they may have missed the first time through.

How: Using a class set of novels or a common text, demonstrate the rereading process. Ask kids to find a spot where they find a detail or moment that they had missed in their first read and rewrite that line on a notebook page. Students then write about how that detail or moment helps them derive more meaning from the story or text.

Writing Connection: Writers should reread their work regularly. Oftentimes kids miss writing down a word, detail, or event. I reread what I have already written—whether in my notebook or on a draft—before I continue. This allows me to fix any glaring editing errors and to add in words or details I may have left out. I often find a sentence that I love or that I didn't write enough about. I'll highlight that line, lift it to another page in my notebook, and begin writing more about it. (Buckner 2005)

Connecting the Unconnected

I love connections. I love the idea of connecting what I read to a zillion different other things. Van de Walle and Lovin (2005) explain that core to understanding a new concept is how kids connect the new information to what they already know. (Ah, schema.) "We use ideas we already have to construct a new idea, developing in the process a network of connections between ideas. The more ideas used and the more connections made, the better we understand" (2005, 2). In reading, connections are important not only to keep children engaged, but to help kids remember what they have read and to make inferences. The more concrete and sound connections they can make, the better the chance is they'll remember what they read.

My kids go crazy with connections. They'll connect to anything. I had gotten frustrated with this and went to the extent of teaching the vocabulary word *irrelevant*. I remember saying, "Boys and girls, if the connection is *irrelevant*—having absolutely nothing to do with the story—you do not need to write it down or share it with the class." I cringe at the thought of having spent time on that. In the new edition of *Strategies That Work* (2007), Harvey and Goudvis have included a lesson about recognizing "distracting connections" and how to refocus ourselves as readers. Some of the connections the kids make may be irrelevant to the text or distracting the reader from the content, but these same connections may be useful for writing. As a teacher of writing, I have a hard time just throwing these connections out. Through my class lessons on connections, I try to model and emphasize the connections that help children understand the story better. However, sometimes in student conferences, I need to be more direct. The following is a conference I held with my student Dean, along with a sample of a connection he made in his writer's notebook.

Aimee: I have been reading your notebook and noticed that you are making connections to your reading.

Dean: Yup.

Aimee: Some of your connections, however, don't seem to go with the meaning of the story or the article you're reading. Have you noticed that?

Dean [*with wide-eyed innocence*]: I have no idea what you're talking about.

Aimee: For example, when we read *The Fairy-Tale Detectives*, I remember the stories the characters come from—like Jack is from "Jack and the Beanstalk."

Dean [*with confidence*]: Text to text.

Aimee: Right. It helps me understand Jack's motive in the story and why he's important. But, when I read about the beanstalk leaf being left behind as a clue in the story and remember that I had green beans for dinner last night, it doesn't really relate to the story.

Dean: Isn't that text to self?

Aimee: It is a text-to-self connection, but do you think it helps me understand the story better or does it just make me think about dinner?

Dean: Well, there might be something about that green bean that could help you.

Aimee: True, and those kinds of connections may lead to some great writing. So, when you find yourself making a connection that may lead to a great story but doesn't really help you out with what you're reading, I want you to put that connection in your writer's notebook for later. We can call it a writer's connection.

Dean: And in my reader's notebook, stick with ideas that help me understand the book, right?

Aimee: That sounds like a good plan. Then if it works for you, you can share this strategy with the class.

Dean [*nodding*]: Got it.

Dean's sample from *The Last Holiday Concert* by Andrew Clements:

LHC:

Text to Self

I have gotten hit by a rubber band before and it hurts! I understand why Mr. M. was mad. OUCH!

 Strategy: Writing Connections

Purpose: To help students quickly sift through connections that may not help them understand the text but that may lead to writing during writing workshop.

How: Although this can be a whole-group lesson or a small-group lesson, I often find I first teach this through a few individual reading conferences. Notice when students' connections are great seed ideas for writing but do not necessarily help their reading. Show the students that these are writing connections and can be placed in their writer's notebooks for later, so that thinking isn't wasted. Then redirect them toward making connections that deepen their thoughts about the text they are reading.

Writing Connection: Writers often get ideas from other books they read. Children do too as they rewrite a favorite story or TV show by simply changing the names. This strategy helps students make deeper connections between their reading and their lives. This teaches students to use favorite stories as springboards for writing rather than retelling the same story.

In a Nutshell: Summarizing

I loved using literature letters as a way for students to respond to their reading. They wrote to me about their book, and I wrote them back with questions to guide their thinking and other book suggestions. I learned this first when I was student teaching and my mentor teacher was reading *Living Between the Lines* by Lucy Calkins with Shelley Harwayne (1990). Fountas and Pinnell revisit the importance of this structure in their comprehensive *Guiding Readers and Writers Grades 3–6: Teaching Comprehension, Genre, and Content Literacy* (2001). Yet each year the same frustrations came—inspired by the same kind of books—but with different kids.

Students would often fill their pages and letters by retelling the story. I must have reread *Harry Potter and the Sorcerer's Stone* (Rowling 1998) a hundred times, as each child who read it retold the many adventures—page after page. It's a great way to kill an otherwise good read. I worked very hard to find an answer to this. Now I often start by generating charts with my class to help them understand the difference between summarizing and retelling (see Figure 3.1). Their explanations always amaze me, make me smile, and sometimes make me laugh. But overall, they *seem* to know the difference.

Figure 3.1

Summarizing is...	Retelling is...
» a recap of what you read.	» telling the story again.
» the highlights of the story.	» giving all the details—as much as you
» the main idea of what you read.	can remember.
» just enough information to make sure the teacher knows you read it.	» telling how things happened in the order they happened.
» telling the beginning and the end without the stuff in the middle.	» saying the story again so the person who hasn't read it feels like they have.
» short, very short.	» more than a summary but less than a book.
	» saying EVERYTHING!

Aimee: Look at these charts. You all have a very good idea of the difference between summarizing and retelling. Which do you think is easier?

Dean: Definitely retelling.

Drew: Yeah, you don't have to think as much.

Aimee: What do you mean, you don't have to think as much?

Drew: Well, it's like carving a turkey at Thanksgiving. When you put the meat on the platter, you have all this meat. It doesn't look like the turkey but you know it's the whole thing—except for the bones. That's retelling—the meat of the story.

Aimee [*almost afraid to ask*]: So what part of the turkey is summarizing?

Drew: That's the part your mom picks out from around the bones to put in soup and stuff. It's just bits and pieces to give you the flavor of the turkey. You don't get the whole turkey or even most of the turkey—just enough to know the flavor. That's the summary. *And* it's a lot more work, because you have to get past all the other meat.

That's a class discussion I won't soon forget. But Drew has a point. The summary gives the flavor of the story, and you have to get through all the other "meat" in order to get those important bits and pieces. It's the thinking through the story, determining the important details, and synthesizing information that make a summary difficult. I love my fourth graders, but if they can figure out a way to write more and think less, they'll do it, because it looks good. Unfortunately for them, I actually read their work, and so I have to continually tell them that less is more. Less writing—more thinking. I'd rather have a one-page entry with a summary and some evidence of their thinking than two or three pages of a retelling. Less is more, and Drew has been heard more than once adding on to that phrase—less is more . . . work. Tough.

A Step Between Retelling
and Summarizing

I referred to Kelly Gallagher's book *Deeper Reading* earlier in this chapter. Kelly is an amazing high school teacher in California, and I use a lot of his ideas for my elementary students. Kelly has a firm grasp of what it means to support children who can read words to extract meaning as the texts get more difficult. Granted he reads Shakespeare's *Romeo and Juliet* and Harper Lee's *To Kill a Mockingbird* with his class, whereas I'm pushing through *Goblins in the Castle* by Bruce Coville and *Every Living Thing* by Cynthia Rylant. The texts aren't quite on the same level, but his ideas for supporting struggling readers are great and easily adapted for younger students.

One of my favorites that he writes about is telling the students ahead of time what is going to happen in the chapter. He lists five or ten events in the order in which they happen as a guide for the students as they read. Sometimes Kelly gets a little crazy and leaves out an event or two to see if the kids catch it. For more difficult reads, it's like a path for the readers to follow.

Since I can select my books for reading, I take into consideration my students' reading levels. This eliminates the need to teach a book that is beyond my students' grasp without a lot of support. It's something I truly love about staying in elementary school. Nonetheless, I figure this strategy is actually a notch between retelling and summarizing. Kelly gives the big ideas in the order they happen (retelling), but he leaves out a lot of the details that surround the events (summary). I've adjusted his strategy to fit the needs of my fourth graders. I call it the Fab Five. Students need to write five sentences about what they read before they continue with their thinking. It can be five retelling sentences, a summary, or anything in between. It can be in a paragraph or a list. I don't care. The catch is—they can use only five sentences.

This proves to be difficult for some, and for others it is freeing. The Fab Five is a way for students to start a notebook entry. Since getting started seems to be the hardest thing for them, this strategy allows them to get back into the story—with five sentences—and then get into their thinking with the rest of their entry.

 Strategy: The Fab Five

Purpose: To help students write about a book or chapter they have read without retelling every single detail.

How: Students begin their entry with five sentences about what they read in the book. It can be a sequence of events, details about one event, or a full summary. The catch is they are limited to five sentences that will help me understand what they read.

Writing Connection: When I confer with students about their writing, they often want to reread their piece instead of talking about it. I will stop them and say, "Give me a Fab Five on your writing so I get the gist of it." It's a great way to start a conference when the student isn't sure what to say. It also reveals what the student hasn't written about or where there may be a weakness in the writing piece.

From Fab Five to Summaries

There is a reason to my madness with five sentences for retelling. It's not a number I pulled out of the air, but it could have been. I'm not one to tell students how long something has to be or how many sentences. But as I have learned from writing professionally, sometimes you get assignments like that. "Aimee, I need 1,000 words on reading private entries in a writer's notebook." Or "Aimee, can you give me two double-spaced pages on a favorite craft lesson?" It happens because sometimes writers write too much or not enough.

So where did the five sentences come from? The summarizing strategy I wrote about in *Notebook Know-How: Strategies for the Writer's Notebook* (2005) has five questions.

Who? Who is the main character? Who are the other important characters?

Wants What? The main character has to want something to make the story interesting. What does the main character want in the story?

But? But what happens? What gets in the way of the character getting what she or he wants? This is the problem of the story. It must eventually be resolved.

So? So what does the character do to try to solve the problem? What works for the character? What doesn't?

Then? And then what happens? How is the problem solved? How does the story end?

We use these questions to help us summarize our own writing. If we can't do this about a piece we're writing, then we need to fill in the missing parts. We use these same *five* questions when learning how to summarize stories we're reading. This works mostly with fiction and some nonfiction texts. As students get used to using the Fab Five, I introduce the summarizing questions. It doesn't matter whether I introduce them in reading or writing first, but I do introduce them in only one workshop at a time to prevent summarizing overload. Eventually, this strategy replaces the Fab Five and my students have a way to summarize efficiently and effectively.

Strategy: *Summarizing Questions*

Purpose: To help students write a summary rather than a retelling when starting a reader's notebook entry about a chapter or book they have read.

How: Introduce and explain the five questions: (1) Who? (2) Wants what? (3) But? (What happens?) (4) So? (What does the character do?) (5) Then? (How does it end?) Students use these questions to help them pick out the kind of details or information they need to write an effective summary.

Writing Connection: This strategy lends itself to writing in paragraphs. As my students begin to use these questions, they often want to write in a question-and-answer format. I model (more than once) how to think the question and write the sentence. Then I move to writing the sentences in a paragraph. The way the questions are ordered lends itself nicely to a paragraph format.

Chapter 4
Reading Like a Writer

As teachers, there is a part of us that is always working. It's true; I'm always on the lookout for a good book or resource for a unit I know I'll teach in the upcoming year. If there is a special museum exhibit, I want to see it and find out the field trip information about it. I read professional books at the pool and look forward to going to conferences. And because I live near where I work, I end up having parent conferences all over town.

Many of us are used to being stopped in the grocery store or at a restaurant by a student who wants to say hello or introduce us to the grandparents. We find ways to stop parent conferences in our driveways or at birthday parties. What I find interesting though, and maybe I shouldn't, is when parents talk to me about other teachers. This doesn't happen often—especially in a negative way—because I've earned a reputation of being a teacher cheerleader. But there is one conversation that stuck with me. I was at a birthday party at a local restaurant and ran into a friend who wanted to ask me about something her child's classroom teacher had said.

"Luke won't stop reading," Heather began. "He reads all the time, and I'm beginning to worry."

"Why?" I asked.

"Well, he reads but he needs to work on his writing. Can you give me any tips?"

"What did his teacher say?"

"She said not to worry. But he'll have to take the fifth-grade writing test in two years! How can I not worry?"

"Let him read," I responded. Noting that from the look on her face she wanted something more, I added, "Try to get him to read more fantasy. It will make him a better writer."

"Really?" Heather is a lawyer, so she kept probing. "Why? Why does reading fantasy help his writing?"

Truthfully, I have absolutely no data on that bit of advice I gave her. I have no idea if reading fantasy helps someone's writing. I do know that kids who write well—really well—tend to read a lot of different genres, including fantasy. My students who don't write as well tend to read more realistic fiction. This advice is kind of like a doctor telling someone with a cold to eat chicken noodle soup. It might help but it definitely won't hurt.

I told Heather all of this and she said, "His teacher told me something about the more he reads the better he'll write. That I should just be patient. I just don't understand how it helps. It makes sense that it would help, but I don't see the actual connection."

Isn't that the truth? Reading to be a better writer makes a lot of sense. Stephen King said, "If you don't have time to read, you don't have the time or tools to write" (2000, 147). And Gary Paulsen's advice to young writers: "Read like a wolf eats" (Cary 1997).

So what is the connection and how do we help students see the bridge between the books they read and the stories they write? In one of the Indiana Jones movies, Indiana has to get from one side of a chasm to the other. Essentially there is a bridge he has to cross, but he can't see it. He has to believe it's there. Once he does, he can see the bridge. The reading-writing connection is not that mystical. It's grounded in theory—theory that, as teachers, we may forget to explain to parents or forget that we know ourselves. However, understanding why this connection is there and how to help others see it and believe it is key to reading like a writer and making that bridge a strong foundation between the two disciplines.

Understanding the Connection

Piaget's work helps us understand that children learn new concepts starting with the concrete before moving to the more abstract. This is hammered into us when learning to teach mathematics—use manipulatives first, then move to the algorithm. It's similar with going from reading to writing. Retelling an event that has happened to a child helps the child take his or her concrete experience and relive it in an abstract way. A book, a story, the words on a page give concrete examples of what stories look like when they're written and how a book works. Then as children develop, they move to the blank page—the abstract—to write their own stories.

The constructivist theory, which builds on Piaget's work, pushes our understanding that children learn from using their environment and schema to interact with new ideas in order to build a new understanding. In relation to reading and writing, we can say that children's experience with books and how stories work allows them to interact with and understand more complex reading. It also helps children create a framework from which they can build their own stories—that is, write.

Vygotsky gave educators the theory of the zone of proximal development, which maintains that children can learn from adult example and gradually accomplish a task or solve a problem without adult assistance. This theory led to the idea of scaffolding within instruction—giving students needed support until they are able to solve problems and perform tasks on their own. In the reading world, this support has been provided by what has become known as the just-right book. Kids need to read books that are not too easy for them, to avoid boredom, but that are not too difficult either, to avoid frustration.

Then looking at Brian Cambourne's Conditions of Learning theory (Rushton, Eitelgeorge, and Zickafoose 2003), we can begin to see how all of this theory builds a very real bridge between reading and writing. Cambourne outlines eight conditions for learning new material: immersion, demonstration, engagement, expectations, responsibility, employment, approximation, response. (See Figure 4.1 for brief definitions of each condition.)

Figure 4.1

Understanding Brian Cambourne's Conditions of Learning

Brian Cambourne's Conditions of Learning	Brief Definition
1. Immersion	Learners need extensive exposure to the subject being taught.
2. Demonstration	Model, model, model. Teachers model behaviors of the subject at hand, and students are given the opportunity to do the same.
3. Engagement	Students need to participate in their learning. Learning experiences should attract the students' attention and involve their thinking and participation.
4. Expectations	Learners respond to high expectations—helping them to envision using the skills in a meaningful way.
5. Responsibility	Learners take on ownership with decisions of what to write, when to write, how to write, and so forth.
6. Employment	Students need opportunities to use what they are learning in an authentic context.
7. Approximation	Students are aware of trying new skills and may not do so perfectly. Learning from their mistakes propels them to further study.
8. Response	Students need positive feedback, constructive redirection, and appropriate encouragement in response to their efforts.

Adapted from Rushton, Eitelgeorge, and Zickafoose (2003) and Lent (2006).

When we read to children and when they read to themselves, we're immersing them in writing of some genre. That's the first reason why when we read a lot we become better writers. As teachers, we point out how writers are using words to paint a picture or create tension.

While studying the Civil War, I read *Henry's Freedom Box: A True Story from the Underground Railroad* (Levine 2007). It's a story about a slave named Henry who mailed himself out of the South to Philadelphia. The story begins in his childhood with his mother reminding him that slaves can be sold at any time. Eventually he's given away to his master's son, and he marries and has a family of his own. When one day his family is sold while he is working in a factory, Henry decides to escape. Enlisting the help of conductors on the Underground Railroad, Henry mails himself in a cargo box to Philadelphia.

I share this story with my students for several reasons—the time period, the adventure and tension in the story, as well as the beautiful pictures. I use parts of this text to demonstrate how an author might build tension in a piece—that kind of feeling where readers seem to hold their breath in anticipation of the character's reaction.

"Boys and girls," I begin, "remember when we read *Henry's Freedom Box?*"

Some students nod and others say yes.

"I want us to look at some parts of this story. There were times, while reading this, that I felt myself holding my breath, waiting to see what would happen. Did anyone else get that feeling?"

"I did," volunteers Drew. "Like when he was on the ship and the men were moving the box around. I was afraid he'd get caught."

"Yeah," pipes in Dean, "I thought the same thing when he ran after his family. What if his master saw him?"

"I'm going to show you some parts where I felt the same way. I want us to read these like a writer—try to discover how the writer created that tension." On the overhead, I show an excerpt from the book:

His friend James came into the factory. He whispered to Henry, "Your wife and children were just sold at the slave market."

"No!" cried Henry.

Henry couldn't move.

He couldn't think.

He couldn't work.

"Twist that tobacco!" The boss poked Henry.

Henry twisted tobacco leaves. His heart twisted in his chest. (17)

Students immediately raise their hands. "I felt myself hold my breath when he found out his wife and children were sold," says Zoe. Many children nod in agreement.

"Notice how the author didn't just say Henry cried out and then immediately the boss poked Henry. What did she do to let us sit in Henry's thoughts for a moment?"

Drew raises his hand halfway, giving me the impression he has a guess but isn't quite sure. I call on him anyway.

"Well, she has three sentences between Henry crying, 'No!' and the boss poking."

"You're right. Let's focus on those three sentences. Read them again to yourself and talk to a partner about what you notice."

I want to give the students time to talk it over with someone else. I've been able to demonstrate how to talk about the text, by narrowing the text down to the specific part I want them to notice. "Okay, what did you or your partner notice?"

Dean raises his hand. "The sentences all have *couldn't*."

Emma replies before I can, "Yes, and notice that they start with *Henry* or *He*. It seems like it's repeating but it's not quite."

"You're right. She starts the sentences in a similar, simple manner and stretches out Henry's feelings for three sentences. One feeling or action in each sentence. Ralph Fletcher calls this slowing down the 'hot spot' (2007, 112). Let me show you an example."

On the easel I write: *I looked up from my book to see Johnny passing a note to Donna. I wanted to snap my fingers. I wanted to raise my voice. I wanted to grab the note from their hands. But I didn't want to disturb the other readers. So I slowly got up and put my hand out palm side up. Donna dropped the note in my hand and her eyes back into her book.*

"Can anyone find where I tried to create tension by slowing down the hot spot?"

"I can!" says Dean. "It's the three sentences after Johnny passed the note."

"You're right."

"And . . . ," continues Zoe, "you have one action in each sentence. So instead of saying you wanted to snap your fingers, raise your voice, and grab the note, you lingered in the moment with each sentence."

Drew looks like a light's going on. "So we can slow writing down by using separate sentences instead of cramming everything into one long sentence?" he asks.

"You got it. Now, when you go to write today, find a spot where you can add tension using this technique. If your writing doesn't lend itself to this, then I want you to do a quick-write and try it before moving on."

This mini-lesson is an example of demonstration. Notice how I'm able to take some literature they have already read and reimmerse them in the story. I then pull a part out to let the author's work demonstrate how to build tension, and use our reactions as readers to find the spot. Then, I model how to use this same technique in my own writing before sending the kids off to try it.

The mini-lesson is a great place for demonstration. I also find this condition of learning present in my conferring and small-group work. As teachers, we naturally use demonstration of how writers work whenever we use literature, our own writing, or student samples.

Using a scaffold approach to demonstrate writing techniques allows students to become more actively engaged in two ways. Students begin to notice in their own reading how writers are demonstrating writing techniques, and students will begin to emulate their favorite authors—trying to write just like them. At this level of engagement, teachers establish expectations for the students. We expect children to notice quality writing, we expect them to try different crafts within their own work, and we expect them to develop their own sense of style. From here, writing improves dramatically, but there is still learning to come. As students take responsibility for these expectations, they will try more difficult or complex things in their writing. And although they may not nail the metaphor the first time, they begin to see their own approximations as stepping-stones toward being a better writer. As children explore these approximations, teachers continue to praise, immerse, and demonstrate in response. This encourages children to keep trying, keep noticing, keep learning more about their own craft of writing.

Katie Wood Ray writes about reading like a writer in her book *Wondrous Words*; she credits Frank Smith with the phrase "reading like a writer" (1999, 15). Smith says, "Teachers must also ensure that children have access to reading materials that are relevant to the kind of writer they are interested in becoming at a particular moment. Teachers must recruit the authors who will become children's unwitting collaborators" (1988, 26). Katie Wood Ray adds to this notion that reading like a writer isn't just about reading good books. It's about reading with a sense of possibility. What's possible to do in my own writing? What is the writer trying to do in this piece? How can it be possible to make this work for a nine-year-old?

This is difficult for children—planning on using a certain writing craft and finding a place for it in their writing. I think many children rely on the literacy spillover—writing like an author they just read because that style is on their mind. There's not anything wrong with this, but it's better if students can be more purposeful, as Ray explained.

So part of reading like a writer means rereading one's own work and finding the spot where the writing needs some help. This takes practice and patience. It's why I usually end my mini-lessons this way: "I want you to try this in your writing today. Reread your work and find a spot where this will help your story. If you don't find a place in your story, do a quick-write in your notebook using this craft before moving on to your other writing." My expectation is that they'll find a place to use it, and this frames some of my conferences with children—teaching them to reread and rework their piece. Reading like a writer extends not only to other people's work—like an author's, the teacher's, or other students'—but to one's own work as well.

Reading like a writer is more complex than just reading, or reading with possibility, or rereading books you love. It's more complex than that, because it's all of those things through the eyes of a writer who is creating a new text. It does not mean students will learn things by accident, nor does it mean that the curriculum is thrown out and kids will just discover something in the books. For all the unknown possibilities that remain out there for young writers, the realm is tightened by a skilled teacher with his or her curriculum in mind. As a classroom teacher, I am mindful that my job is to teach the curriculum, but how I teach it remains in my hands. Using the theories that build the bridge between reading and writing and Katie Wood Ray's structures for reading like a writer, I have found ways to make peace with both the curriculum and the independence of each writer. But it all starts with reading . . . from the very beginning.

From Noticing to Practicing

I remember when I first started trying literature circles in my classroom. I taught the children how to do each job from Discussion Director and Illustrator to Word Wizard and Summarizer (Daniels 2002). My favorite, though, was Literary Luminary. I loved this job for two reasons: first, I liked to say the phrase *literary luminary*, and second, this was the job that required readers to react to the writing in the book—to highlight a phrase they liked or a paragraph that took their breath away. In essence, the work of Harvey Daniels and others gave us a way to help children read like a writer.

So why is this important for readers to do? Why is reading like a writer in a book about writing about reading? It's because readers who are not aware of their own thinking while reading are rarely aware of the writing style they're reading. But readers who think, readers who are aware of how a story is put together, and readers who notice the way words make them feel—these are the readers who turn into writers. It's part of the bridge between the two disciplines. We can't look at the writing of a piece if we haven't read it as a reader first. Likewise, we can't read a piece to look at the writing if we can't understand what is written. In order to get to the writing part, we have to read with metacognition.

When students are learning to notice what a writer does, it usually happens when they're reading. We look at parts that take our breath away, make us laugh, or make us cry. These are the parts of a story that we want to reread and figure out how the writer did that. Because it is from here that we can start thinking about how we can make our own readers lose their breath, laugh out loud, or even cry.

When my students are ready to look at a writer's writing because they want to write that way, we actually switch notebooks. We move from our reader's notebooks to our writer's notebooks. Students do not have to do this—they can keep it all in their reader's notebooks. I'm aware that many teachers like to have only one notebook for both reading and writing. That's fine too. There isn't one right answer to which notebook a child should use or how many notebooks a child should have for reading and writing. I usually advise teachers to think about what makes sense to them. If one notebook for reading and writing works, then go for it. If two separate notebooks work for you, then have two notebooks. If you want reading-like-a-writer stuff in the reader's notebook, the more power to you. It's really a matter of organization and what makes sense for you and your students. However, since my students keep two separate notebooks, most of them find this next step—practicing what we notice—is better suited to their writer's notebook.

When I begin to teach students how to notice and practice what they learn from authors, I often begin with a whole-class exploration. I choose excerpts from texts that we have already read, excerpts from texts that can stand alone, or short stories and vignettes. Although I have many favorites for this task, I find that using an excerpt from the classic book

Maniac Magee by Jerry Spinelli (1990) allows students to utilize several different comprehension strategies while at the same time inviting them to try several different things in their writing.

I use this excerpt frequently with my students and other teachers. It's one of those where the kids do not have to read the whole book to wring some value from it. I usually type a copy for children to glue in their writer's notebook, so they can mark what they notice as the passage is read and reread. I also have a copy on the overhead projector to mark as the class discussion progresses.

Note: When students are reading on their own and notice interesting writing in their books, they usually record that in the reader's notebook. This is because at that point it is an extension of their own reading and how they're making sense of the text. Generally, this "literary luminary" part of their reading is really extending what they understand about the text and thereby recognizing that as a well-written part. When students take a closer look at an excerpt—whether it's one they've chosen or one I've selected—out of the context of the entire story, they will move to their writer's notebooks. Using the excerpt generally signals that we're going to dig deeper into how the author wrote it and how this can help us as writers. Also, when I want students to use an excerpt to specifically focus on the writing of it, it's helpful to be in the writer's notebook so that they can try the techniques immediately in their own writing.

Clear as mud yet? The biggest difference is that, unless the students write it down while reading on their own, the passage is *not* usually included in the reader's notebook and it is in the writer's notebook. Second, in the reader's notebook the student focuses on constructing meaning to understand the text, whereas in the writer's notebook the focus is on how the writer created the text and the effect it has on a reader. Ultimately, it really doesn't matter where all of this goes—reader's notebook or writer's notebook. It's more of an organizational decision than a philosophical one.

"Boys and girls, I want you to read along silently as I read this passage aloud. I don't want you to do anything but listen. Then I'll read the text again. When I read it through the second time, you can begin marking the passage where you like the way the author wrote about something. Then I'll give you time to reread the passage to yourself a third time. I'll give you some time to think and mark the passage, and then we'll talk about it."

Summer raises her hand. "Ms. Buckner, when we mark the passage, can we use our highlighter?"

"Yes. You can use a highlighter, but you don't have to," I respond as several students go digging in their desks for highlighters.

Summer raises her hand again. "Do we underline, highlight, or circle?"

"You can mark the text any way you want. I find it helpful to write notes off to the side to remind myself about what I was thinking when I marked a certain word or phrase."

And so I begin. I read the piece once, entirely, then reread it as children start marking the text. (See an example in Figure 4.2.) And finally I give them about three to five minutes to reread and continue thinking about the writing of this piece.

Figure 4.2

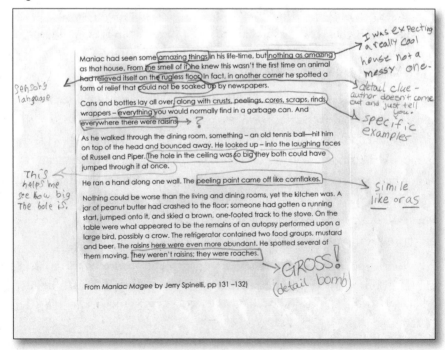

It's important for children to hear stories or excerpts more than once if we want them to think about the writing aspect of the story. As readers, when we read a story, we focus on the context of the story first. So readers usually need two to three—if not more—readings before they can begin to notice the workings of the writer. I see this with myself as each year, if and when I reuse a passage, I notice something different. This further cements the need for rereading with my students as a normal thing readers and writers do.

When the kids are ready, I ask them to come up to the front and mark the text that I have on the overhead projector. Each child then explains why he or she marked that part of the text. Kids love coming up to the overhead, so this encourages participation. Also, for those who are struggling, this gives an extra support, because they can see and hear what others have done. It's perfectly legal to "borrow" ideas off the overhead and mark it on their own paper.

Here is how one class marked up the excerpt:

Maniac had seen some amazing things in his lifetime, but nothing as amazing as that house.

Student comment: This sentence really grabbed me. It's a grabber lead.

The peeling paint came off like cornflakes.

Student comment: I could see this in my mind. It's a simile.

Nothing could be worse than the living and dining rooms, yet the kitchen was.

Student comment: This grabbed my attention. It's like another grabber lead, but it's not at the beginning.

autopsy

Student comment: ?????

They weren't raisins; they were roaches.

Student comment: GROSS!

I try not to interrupt as students volunteer to come up and talk about the piece. Unless a student misidentifies something, I let them do the talking and then respond afterward.

"You all noticed a lot of things. I'm really impressed," I begin. "How many marked the first line as a grabber lead?" Hands go up. "It seems like that, but this piece is in the middle of the book. It's not even the lead sentence of a chapter."

"Really!" Summer is shocked. "So it's like a regrabber lead—a sentence to regrab the reader's attention?"

"You could say that. It's also called a transition sentence, because it leads the reader from one topic in the story to a new one. Can you find another transition sentence?"

"Well, that sentence about the living and dining rooms being bad but not as bad as the kitchen . . . That seemed to move us to another room and grabbed our attention again," says Drew.

"You're right. So that might be something you can try in the middle of your stories—regrab your reader's attention with an interesting transition sentence."

"What about that raisin thing?" asks Emma. "I was like, huh? Raisins? What's he talking about? Then I forgot about them and at the end they're really roaches. That's so gross!"

"It's like a detail you pass up in the beginning but then it like . . . explodes at the end," adds Drew.

"I'm not really sure what you call that writing technique," I respond honestly, "but I see what you mean."

"We can call it a detail bomb," says Drew. "At first it just sits there and then it explodes!" He laughs and the boys join in. I think they think they have zapped the teacher.

"Actually, Drew, I like that, and I think you're right. Even though we don't write about violence in school, there's nothing wrong with setting off a detail explosion in our writing. We'll call it a detail bomb.

"Now, here's the catch. We noticed a lot of things about Jerry Spinelli's writing today. You now have two jobs and I'm going to write them on this chart paper so you don't forget."

Reading Like a Writer: From Notebook to Notebook

As a reader:

» Stop yourself when you have read a really great part of a book.

» Go back and reread the same part two or three times.

» What do you notice the writer did to help you enjoy the piece as a reader?

» Record this in your reader's notebook as you read.

As a writer:

» Try to use some of the techniques you notice when you write in your writer's notebook.

» Make a quick note to yourself about what you're trying to do so we can talk about it later.

Here are some samples I found from reader's and writer's notebooks that show how students might approach this strategy differently in the two notebooks.

Student Sample: Dean

Reader's Notebook: Dean lifted a line from the book *Goblins in the Castle* by Bruce Coville (1992). After the quote, he wrote more about it.

"Don't put foot in water, might not get it back."

I think there must be something dangerous in the water. If William puts his foot in the water, will something eat it? I think it's a surprising sentence because I go to the lake all the time and nothing bites me in the water.

Writer's Notebook: trying grabber lead in the middle of a story. Here Dean is inspired by two pieces of writing. He wanted to try the Jerry Spinelli technique of a grabber lead within a paragraph. He also tried to add some mystery and surprise, inspired by *Goblins in the Castle*, in his lake story.

Once I was at Lake Lanier. We were on our houseboat. I saw this little girl on her houseboat. She fell off. She screamed, HELP! HELP! Two men jumped in the water to save her. She went down really fast, like a shark was pulling her under. No one has found that little girl. So pay close attention to the water, because something might grab you.

This excerpt from Dean's writer's notebook shows how he is making a deliberate attempt at using a grabber lead (transition) within a story. Although he writes a great sentence that adds to the drama of his story, it's not quite what he had set out to do. It's an approximation—well within the conditions of learning. My response to him is positive, and I redirect him to try it again on a notebook entry that has less drama and could use a grabber-lead sentence in the middle of it.

Student Sample: Summer

Reader's Notebook: Summer responded to *This Is the Tree: A Story of the Baobab* by Miriam Moss (2005) after I read it to the class and she had time to reread it.

I like the rhythm of this book. It's like a long poem. I like how each little part is about one thing with lots of details. It helped me visualize the small parts of the tree that add up to a very busy place!

Writer's Notebook: using prepositional phrases to add detail; using a repeating line. Inspired by *This Is the Tree: A Story of the Baobab*.

> *This is my room*
>
> *with a big warm bed,*
>
> *that I come to every night.*
>
> *This is my room,*
>
> *with a walk-in closet*
>
> *where my new clothes hang.*
>
> *This is my room*
>
> *that is quiet and peaceful.*
>
> *I love to look outside.*
>
> *This is my room*
>
> *where my dog loves to hide*
>
> *after a bath.*

Summer does a great job adapting the rhythm, repetition, and use of prepositional phrases to her own writing. Although there is a part that moves away from the established pattern ("This is my room that is quiet and peaceful. I love to look outside"), most of it is quite charming. In response to her efforts, I congratulate her on writing. I also point out that Miriam Moss uses verbs to make her tree come alive. I redirect Summer to read like a writer, again, to look at Moss's use of verbs to see what she can discover.

I used to get excited when my students would try something they noticed in another author's writing. I didn't worry about whether they actually achieved what they set out to do. Like Dean's work, for example; I would be so excited about the sentence he wrote in the middle of the paragraph that I'd forget to notice if he accomplished what he had set out to do. Cambourne's Conditions of Learning remind me that I can get excited about the students' approximations, but it's also my job to redirect writers so they can try again.

It's Okay to Play Favorites

I was watching my students play at recess on the playground behind our school. Kids were scattered on the basketball court, the slides, and the monkey bars. There was a group of girls walking around, and they seemed to be huddled around one girl in particular. She was deciding who was her BFF, her VBFF, and her VBBFF. In layman's terms—her best friend forever, her very best friend forever, and her very best, best friend forever. No doubt, there were hurt feelings by the end of recess over who was the least favorite best friend.

We all want to be the favorite. The favorite child, friend, teacher, parent . . . being the favorite means being the best. And who doesn't like to be pointed out in such a positive light? As a parent, I'm careful not to have a favorite child, and my mom would always say she didn't have a favorite among her three children. As a teacher, I'm also careful not to have a favorite student. Having a favorite means choosing one person or thing over another. And when it comes to human relationships, that's not a good thing. When it comes to books, well . . . that's business.

All writers have favorite authors. It's a fact. Just like musicians listen to other people's music, authors read other people's writing. I have favorite picture book authors, favorite nonfiction authors, favorite fantasy authors, favorite adult authors, and so forth. I've categorized my favorites, and if I made a list it would look like an awards ceremony. (For a partial list, see Figure 4.3.) So many books, so little time.

Having a favorite author is an essential tool for teaching writing, and I start that teaching by telling my students about writers I admire. I start with Julius Lester. I'm a *huge* fan of his work. I've read the Caldecott Award–winning book *John Henry* more times than I can count. And each time I read it, each time I immerse myself in the words of this timeless classic, Lester teaches me something about writing.

Figure 4.3

Aimee's Favorites

Author	Title	Favorite . . .	Writing Technique to Look For
Julius Lester	*John Henry*	Folktale Author	* Sentence structure * Similes * Use of verbs
Kevin Henkes	*Lilly's Purple Plastic Purse* and *Chrysanthemum*	Picture Book Author	* Main idea with three details * Short, quick sentences to highlight details * Sentence flow
Elizabeth Friedrich	*Leah's Pony*	Historical Fiction Picture Book Author	* Passing time * Repetition * Effective fragments
Michael Buckley	*The Fairy-Tale Detectives*	Fantasy– Fairy Tale Author	* Attention to reader's schema * Establishing setting * Play on words equals connotation
Stephen Kramer	*Lightning* and *Caves*	Nonfiction Picture Book Author	* Lead sentences * Clever subheadings * Use of verbs
Kathleen Krull	*Harvesting Hope* and *Houdini*	Biography Picture Book Author	* Passing time * Writing small * Character development
Russell Freedman	*Indian Chiefs* and others	Biography Author	* Leads * A story within a story * Setting the scene

I was at an NCTE (National Council of Teachers of English) conference, standing in line to get some books signed by Julius Lester. At the time, he was the cutest old man I had ever seen, with his coffee-colored skin, dark graying hair, and glasses that made him look scholarly. As he signed, he laughed and talked with the people in line.

The woman ahead of me turned and asked, "Do you know anything about this author? I have to introduce him at his next session, and I don't know anything about him."

"Are you kidding?" I replied. "That's Julius Lester. Author of several award-winning books, including my favorite, *John Henry*."

A blank look remained stuck on this woman's face.

"He's fabulous." I went on to tell her the bit I knew about his background and that he was a mentor to the students in my class.

"How's that?" she asked as we moved up in line. Not knowing Julius Lester was within earshot, I began to tell her what I have learned about writing from his books. I told her about how he uses sentence structure and length to create tension or to relieve it. I told her how he uses literary devices like alliteration and similes—Ferret Faced Freddy who has a laugh like bat wings on tombstones. I told her how he creates imagery with nouns and verbs and just sprinkles in an adjective here or there. I was on a roll when I noticed Julius Lester was listening to us, shaking his head, and laughing.

"I didn't realize I was doing all that!" he cried. "I'm glad someone is getting something out of these books."

The fact is, much of the time writers write well because of the influence other writers have on them. Brian Cambourne refers to this as "linguistic spillover" (cited in Anderson 2005, 18). It's the effect that happens when we read really wonderful text and then begin to write that way.

 **Strategy:** Favorite Authors

Purpose: Having a favorite author is like having a personal writing mentor. Students don't mind rereading their favorite books, and this opens them up to reading like a writer.

How: Think about your favorite stories to share with the class. Read some and tell the kids why you love the books. Invite the children to bring in and share a favorite book by an author they enjoy. Very quickly, your class will build up a repertoire of favorite authors and books.

Writing Connection: Writers read and reread favorite texts and the work of their favorite authors. As children begin to identify books and authors they love, encouraging them to reread will aid in the literacy spillover effect that Brian Cambourne talks about.

After rereading, students may write in their writer's notebook about the things they notice or like about the book or the author's style.

Lola Schaefer, an author and friend of mine, mentored me on a manuscript I was writing about a cat who catches a thief. Her first bit of advice to me, after I wrote the first draft, was to gather all the cat stories I could and read them. Read them over and over. Get to know the syntax and rhythms authors use when writing a cat character. Listen to the cadence of the words; collect catlike words and phrases to include. Research the writing that's already out there and allow it to influence yours. Helpful advice for any writer. If it's good enough for the professionals, it must be good enough for my students.

Once you have a favorite author in mind, read his or her books. (You can do this with more than one author.) Choose a few books to know well. I have taught full years of writing based on just a few books I knew well. As I developed as a writing teacher, my knowledge of books increased. But it took time to get there, and that's okay. It's okay to use one book to model a great lead sentence, the same book to model productive dialogue, and still the same book to demonstrate the use of active verbs. There is no law that says you have to know a lot of different books. But, if you're an overachiever or you just like variety, then know three writing things about each book you use. Using the same book to teach different elements demonstrates to students that authors use more than one technique of good writing. It also helps children to know a book (or author) well enough to draw from it when trying to emulate the author's writing style.

In the beginning of the year, I read my favorites to my students so that they can enjoy the stories. I keep the books available for kids to reread on their own. And, of course, throughout the year I'll reread the books to point out writing styles and techniques. In this way, I plant the seeds of good writing. I plant the story in their mind and let kids respond to it as readers, to enjoy it as readers, to bring their own experiences to the text so they might remember the story long after the book is closed. It's only later that I use these books for modeling writing. And this is when we cross the bridge—from the reader's notebook to the writer's notebook. When we are rereading specifically as writers—looking at the text to see how the author wrote it and how it might apply to our own writing—we are responding in our writer's notebooks.

As I mentioned earlier, there are many teachers out there who have students keep one notebook for reading and writing. It all goes together in one place. If that makes sense to you, then it's a great idea. As I also mentioned, I'm more of a separatist. Despite the interconnections between the two disciplines, I need two separate places to record the different ways we look at text—as a reader in the reader's notebook and as a writer in the writer's notebook. Each year there are some kids who just start putting everything into one notebook, and if students do that naturally and it makes sense to them, I don't interfere. I find most children cannot change their thinking stance as easily as one notebook would require. Therefore, switching notebooks is like a signal for them to switch the way they are reading the text—from a reader to a writer or vice versa.

Three Things to Know About

When I speak at conferences, I often get a panicked look from the teachers in the audience when I talk about using authors as mentors for writing.

Many teachers do not feel they know enough about writing to teach from trade books. Others don't feel that they know many books well, and they begin to feel overwhelmed with the task of reading stacks and stacks of books to find the "gem."

Here is a secret I share with them: Start with what you know. All of us have a favorite book, so that's where you start. Reading like a writer requires rereading the same book or text over and over again. Readers need to know the story well enough, so that when they read the text, they can admire and notice the way the writing is put together. Sometimes as I'm pushed for time, I forget that my students need to read a story for the sake of the story before they can begin to think more deeply about it. What I try to do, before my students read like a writer or before I use an excerpt as a mentor text, is find three things about a text that I really like. Then I know I'm ready to use the book in class. The kids will surely notice more about the text, which builds my repertoire for teaching. Here are some things to know about some of my favorite books.

John Henry by Julius Lester (1994)

1. On the dedication page, Julius Lester wrote a note that John Henry brings the image of Martin Luther King, Jr. to his mind. This is a classic example of metaphor—the whole book is a metaphor for MLK's life as having "the courage to hammer until our hearts break and to leave our mourners smiling in their tears" (iii).

2. Lester uses personification throughout the text, but most notably in the beginning when he refers to the sun and the moon: "The sun yawned, washed its face, flossed and brushed its teeth, and hurried up over the horizon" (4).

3. Lester compares and contrasts throughout the text. Not only does he use similes to compare, but he also structures his paragraphs to create comparisons. Notice how Lester starts the following paragraph with sentences focused on a steam machine that cuts rocks. Then, toward the end of the paragraph, Lester mentions our hero, John Henry.

What he saw was a mountain as big as hurt feelings. On one side was a big machine hooked up to hoses. It was belching smoke and steam. As the machine attacked the mountain, rocks and dirt and underbrush flew into the air. On the other side was John Henry. Next to the mountain he didn't look much bigger than a wish that wasn't going to come true. (23)

Notice how the first part of the paragraph uses phrases like *big machine, belching smoke and steam, attacked the mountain, rocks and dirt and underbrush flew.* Not only does Julius Lester use phrases that make the machine seem powerful, but he actually gives more sentences to the machine in the paragraph than to John Henry. By doing this, Lester gives the reader the impression that there is no way John Henry can beat this machine. It would be ridiculous to even think so. He hammers this point in as he talks about John Henry: "On the other side was John Henry. Next to the mountain he didn't look much bigger than a wish that wasn't going to come true" (23).

Lester uses only two sentences—the first is very short and merely mentions John Henry. The comparison he uses is a wish that wasn't going to come true. He sets the reader up to think there is no way a mere man could break through the mountain like a machine that can attack. This makes the victory all the sweeter to the reader when John Henry eventually breaks through the mountain.

Julius Lester may not have realized he had done this as specifically as I have pointed it out. Yet he did purposefully set up the reader to believe it would be a miracle if John Henry succeeded. Lester wanted the reader to leave the book believing anything is possible—mountains can be moved.

This Is the Tree: A Story of the Baobab by Miriam Moss (2005)

1. This text is written as a poem, yet it gives plenty of facts about the Baobab tree. The author writes about one thing in each stanza—first the roots of the tree and then the squirrels who sleep among the roots on the ground.

This is the tree with thousand year roots

that spread out to store water

in a bottle-shaped trunk.

This is the tree where ground squirrel watches

over young, small as mushrooms,

asleep in the roots. (4)

2. A poetic device that can work in prose as well is the use of repetition. A good use of repetition has a purpose behind it. Throughout the text in this book, Moss repeats the line "This is the tree . . ." She wants to keep her reader mindful that there is a lot to know about the tree, so as she tells one bit in each stanza, she redirects her readers' attention to the whole tree before she tells the next little bit.

3. Notice how Moss uses prepositional phrases to lengthen her sentences and to give more details to help readers envision the tree.

This is the tree that bushbaby burgles,

plucking white, waxy petals

with *fingers and toes.*

This is the tree that dances with monkeys,

alive with their leapings

at *the end of the day.* (15)

Leah's Pony by Elizabeth Friedrich (1999)

1. Notice how Elizabeth Friedrich passes time in the text:

> *The year the corn grew tall and straight,*
> *Leah's papa bought her a pony.* (1)

> *The year the corn grew no taller than a man's thumb,*
> *Leah's house became very quiet.* (3)

Instead of trying to skip right to the difficult times of the Dust Bowl, Friedrich establishes a summer of growth and prosperity. Also, by simply describing the growth of corn, she's able to pass time on the calendar as well as through seasons.

2. Notice how Friedrich writes in groups of threes. She often shows how the dust storms are affecting the three main characters: Leah, Mama, and Papa.

> *Some days the wind blew so hard it turned the sky black with dust. It was hard for Leah to keep her pony's coat shining. It was hard for Mama to keep the house clean. It was hard for Papa to carry buckets of water for the sow and her piglets.* (3)

3. Notice how Friedrich uses sentence structure to create tension within the story. In this excerpt, Leah's family farm is being auctioned. Leah bids a dollar for her father's tractor. The last three sentences create the tension. The author uses the same words to begin each sentence and then makes the sentence a little longer each time—stretching the tension.

> *It was time. Leah's voice shook, "One dollar."*
>
> *The man in the big hat laughed. "That's a low starting bid if I ever heard one," he said. "Now let's hear some serious bids."*
>
> *No one moved. No one said a word. No one even seemed to breathe.* (9)

Reading like a writer allows students to make purposeful decisions about how they want to craft their writing. Sometimes what they have in mind comes out even better than they thought it would. Sometimes it doesn't. As teachers, we need to honor these attempts while encouraging students to move closer to the actual technique. By reading together as a class and discussing excerpts together, students and teacher can learn side by side. And no one has to know it all before they try something new.

Chapter 5
Beneath the Story: Discovering Hidden Layers

A few years ago, I started asking teachers what kinds of things their students put in their reader's notebooks. I asked out of true curiosity, because at this point—as I noted in Chapter 1—my students' notebooks felt blah. I wanted to learn and find out what others did. I'd get weary looks, as if I was setting the teacher up. I'd have to explain, almost every time I asked, that I didn't feel my reader's notebooks were all that great and I was really interested in learning what other teachers were doing. After a sigh of relief, I'd get similar answers—literature letters, literature-circle jobs, and guided-reading notes.

What about comprehension strategies? How did teachers implement writing about those in the notebooks? Many said prompts. Many said that the whole class worked on a specific strategy together and then wrote about it. Mostly it was done under teacher direction or it appeared in the literature letters. Okay, so my notebooks weren't so far off. But why, then, did they feel blah to me? I felt like I was cheating by "pushing my students' thinking" with prompts (Calkins et al. 2007) or open-ended sentences. It's something I'd have to come to terms with or figure out how to move beyond. I went back to what I know well, writing.

When I write, I often have the whole story or book in mind. I think through the beginning, middle, and end before I start. I do most of this kind of work in my mind, in my notebook, and through talking with friends or editors. It's a ritual for me that lasts a while, much to my editor's chagrin. But once I'm ready, once I know what I want to write and how to write it, I'm off.

Most of us don't do that much preparation when we read, though. We read the blurb of a book, or rely on a favorite author or a friend's recommendation. Some of us read anything Oprah picks out or only award winners. We all have our own path to lead us to books we enjoy. And without much further ado, we read them.

I've begun to notice that many adult books now come with reading-group discussion guides at the back, which include questions to prompt people's thinking, to guide discussion, to help the reader stop and read more deeply into the book. I love this—when the questions are good and not trivial—because if I'm not reading a book for a discussion group, I feel like I have someone else there guiding my thinking and pointing things out I may not have noticed if I just read the book.

It is here that I revamp my position on prompts. In writing, I'm still dead-set against them, with the exception of assessment-related situations beyond the teacher's control. In reading, I've worked hard to steer away from prompts, and many of the strategies have helped me—as a teacher—to guide student thinking without actually telling them what to think about specifically. Yet, when I think about how much I truly love learning and seeing something in a book I wouldn't have seen without the reader's guide in the back, or when I remember how much I truly loved my college literature class and reading a classic with someone who really knew the book inside out, I want to share that joy of discovery with my students. And the reality is, if I don't always see everything there is to see in a book, it's likely my fourth graders won't either.

And so, while thinking about and preparing to write this book, I've come to terms with prompts—of sorts. Of course, I prefer the term *reader's guide*—strategies to guide a reader through a specific genre or book. This requires more thinking and planning on my part. I rarely, if ever, read a book with my class or a group that I haven't read myself. It's a warning I was given early on in my teaching, but one many teachers ignore. The strategies in this chapter would be very difficult to use with an unknown book. I also have had to study more about genre—understanding the underwriting of the book, the structure of how the book should go, and the patterns that unfold. Katie Wood Ray's books *Study Driven* (2006) and *Wondrous Words* (1999) have been very helpful with this. Finally, I've had to be prepared to lift questions from class conversations instead of preparing prompts for my students to answer.

Connotation

Inferring is a difficult strategy to teach students. It requires students to use their background knowledge and clues from the text in order to create their own meaning. We infer when we visualize, read body language, and anticipate someone's actions. We all infer—daily and quite naturally. So drawing attention to it and putting directions to it often confuses children and makes this concept difficult to grasp. Yet, there are many, many strategies we can use to help children become more aware of when they infer.

According to *Webster's Online Dictionary*, the word *connotation* is a noun meaning "a. the suggesting of a meaning by a word apart from the thing that it explicitly names or describes or b. something suggested by a word or thing—an implication." Let me give you an example from *Holes* by Louis Sachar (2000). This novel opens up with the main character, a boy, riding on a bus to Camp Green Lake. Sachar relies on the reader's schema of *camp* to mean something fun and wonderful for kids to do during the summer. He lulls the reader into a false sense of security and then slowly reveals that this is not an ordinary camp—and to the reader's surprise this camp is a prison camp, not a fun camp.

The word *camp* used in the setting he sets up gives the connotation, implies, that this child is off for a fun summer. Sachar never says that; the reader brings that to the book, which is one reason it's so good.

What about the word *dreams*? What do you think about when you hear that word? I often get responses such as "Dreams are when you sleep" or "daydreaming during class." Sometimes I get responses linking dreams to goals one may have. Depending on how the word is used, it can have different meanings, and a skilled author can use it to imply something altogether different.

Dreams

by Langston Hughes

Hold fast to dreams
For if dreams die
Life is a broken-winged bird
That cannot fly.

Hold fast to dreams
For if dreams go
Life is a barren field
Frozen in snow.

In this poem, this dream of Langston Hughes's (1994, 4) is not just a dream at night or a goal for himself. It's more on the level of Martin Luther King, Jr.'s dream. The poem with its simple title transcends our first understanding of the word *dreams* and takes the reader to a whole new level of thought. This is the power of a word—this is the power of connotation in the hands of a skilled writer.

As a teacher of upper elementary school students, I realize it is unlikely they'll pick this up on their own while reading. It requires inferring, and the more attention I give that strategy in my reading workshop, the more kids are aware of when they infer. Sometimes I'll have a student say she or he was surprised Camp Green Lake was a prison and not a fun camp. But more often than not, kids blow by this subtle vocabulary technique. So I've put this in my "reader's guide" collection of lessons. It's a strategy I guide kids through to help elevate their thinking about a certain text.

While working through *The Comprehension Toolkit* by Stephanie Harvey and Anne Goudvis (2005), my class was reading and responding to "At Home in the Arctic." We were practicing how to set up our reading with questions based on the title, headings, and pictures of a nonfiction text. I was working with third graders and some of the questions were what I expected.

Who lives in the Arctic?

How do they live in the Arctic?

Do only polar bears live in the Arctic?

How can you live in the Arctic without plants?

How do polar bears stay warm? Do they like the cold?

Finally, Alex said, "I don't like this title."

"Why not?" I asked.

"Well, the Arctic isn't my idea of being homey," she said.

We immediately shifted our focus from setting up questions to guide our reading and started talking about the word *home* and its connotation for the reader. This is important, because the author did this on purpose.

"Okay, let's think about this," I said, pulling up another piece of chart paper and writing the word *home* at the top. "What do you think about when you hear the word *home?*"

"I think about being warm and safe," said Alex. "We have blankets and an alarm system."

I wrote *warm, safe* on the chart paper. "Anyone else?"

"I think of my bedroom and the toys I have there," said Jeremy.

I wrote *my room* and *toys* on the chart paper.

"My mom making dinner," shouted out Charlie.

And the responses continued until we had a chart full of ideas about home that didn't match the Arctic at all. At least not yet . . . "So," I continued, trying to connect this back to our article, "when we think of the word *home*, none of us thinks of being cold, walking on ice, and living in the Arctic. I think the author knew we might have a different idea of *home*. This is called *connotation*, when an author uses a word that will make us think one way but he or she means it in a different way. When you read this article, we have a lot of questions to think about," I said as I referred to our questioning chart. "But now we also have this new question—how does the idea of *home* fit in with what we know about the Arctic?"

Here is Rachel's thinking from our conversation after reading the article.

Background knowledge: Home is a place I live. It's shelter for my family and animals. I have plants and it's very comfortable. The Arctic is cold and frozen. There are some animals but people don't live there. I don't think there are any plants—just ice. Brrr!

?? How does the word home connect to the Arctic if no one lives there??

Polar bears live in the Arctic. "Ah, home freezing home!" They must have a lot of fur and like the cold weather. People and other animals can't live there, because they would be freezing! Polar bears are "home" in the Arctic, how can they be comfortable? It turns out polar bears have black skin that keeps them warm and two layers of fur. Wow. This is like wearing two heavy coats, so polar bears must be hot, not cold. Polar bears get all of their needs—food, shelter, and warmth there. I guess it is home for them.

And here is Alex's response.

We were wondering how home and arctic connect, because people don't live there and it doesn't seem very warm or safe. One I figured out that it is where polar bears live, I know it's there home. How is it safe, though? I have an alarm system, but since humans don't live in the arctic, it's safer for polar bears to live there. No alarm system needed! Plus baby seals live in the water up there. And guess what? That's the polar bear's favorite food. It's like a living refrigerator under the bear's feet! Polar bears love the arctic. It's their home.

 Strategy: Connotation

Purpose: To point out to students that authors may use words that make readers think one thing but really mean another. This helps keep readers engaged and surprises them as they figure out what the author is actually talking about in the text.

How: Introduce the concept of connotation with the poem "Dreams" by Langston Hughes. First ask what students think about when they hear the word *dreams*. Note the variety or lack of variety of answers. Then read the poem. (Have a copy for each student or have it on chart paper for all to see.) Ask students what kind of dream Hughes is referring to and explain that sometimes writers use a word in a different way than readers expect. (Other sources can include *Holes* by Louis Sachar and "At Home in the Arctic" in *The Comprehension Toolkit* by Stephanie Harvey and Anne Goudvis.)

Writing Connection: In their writer's notebooks, students may want to start collecting words that have more than one meaning. Then as they write, they may try to use a word in a way that implies one thing but means another. Some words to start with may include *dreams, home, camp, counselor, party.*

Theme

I have a friend who is a whiz at online dating. It turns out, you can go to these various websites and put in a keyword and out pops Romeo! So if you love to read, you type in the word *read* or *books* and a catalog of men who actually claim to read pops up. Interesting. The same thing is true for other sites that allow searches—even searches for books. You can put in the word *friend* and out pops a list of books about friendship. Or you can type in *World War II* and out pops that list. It makes me wonder, how does the computer know? Well, clearly, someone has read the book—usually an editor—and pulled out keywords identified with the book's theme.

Most books have a theme of some sort—a concept or message threaded throughout the book. As a student in high school and college, I was often given the task of identifying the book's central theme and then writing an essay defining and defending the theme. It wasn't always easy, and my ideas didn't always match the "right" answer.

For elementary students, they can understand the idea of theme, but we're often in such a hurry to move on to the next book or the next objective that we don't have time for hindsight—thinking about a book after we read it. I've begun to undo that hurry and have really hooked into the idea of studying a book—rereading and discussing the book before, during, and after we read it. As a class, we may read fewer books together, but we're reading and thinking more deeply than I ever thought possible with nine-year-olds.

I do cheat a bit though. I give them a keyword before they read the book. I usually have several keywords that they can choose from, and their job is to think about how that one word resonates throughout the book. In their reader's notebooks, or on sticky notes or a thinkmark, students keep track of ideas and events that happen that connect to their keyword. In essence, they follow a theme, which guides their thinking as they read. This often requires the kids to reread parts of the book on their own, as they try to get the story in mind as well as the underlying theme.

While reading aloud *The Last Holiday Concert* by Andrew Clements (2006), I gather some of my students to try out this strategy.

"What do you think about our book so far?" I ask.

"I love it!" says Drew. "I think the teacher is mean, though."

Emma agrees. "Yeah, I don't like the teacher either. He doesn't make things fun. But I don't think Hart should have shot the rubber bands."

"It was an accident," Drew reminds her.

"I don't think so. What did he expect to happen if he was playing with rubber bands?" Emma retorts.

Before the conversation goes too far down this road, I interrupt. "Well, I think we're just talking about the story and not really thinking deeply about what we're reading. But I have an idea!"

"You always do," chimes in Trey, always the charmer.

"I have read this book before, and I think there are some words that may help us reveal some deeper ideas in the story. They're like a magnifying glass—by reading the book with one of these words in mind, it will help you see things others might miss."

"What kind of words?" Emma asks suspiciously.

"I have four: *popularity, peace, self-centered,* and *control.*"

"What are we supposed to do?" asks Katelyn.

"I'm glad you asked. I want you to choose a word; then you're going to work with a partner to think about the word and its meaning, and then as you read, you're going to think about how your word connects to this book and story."

We try it together with the word *self-centered.* We first discuss what it means to be self-centered and how that might be described. Then we talk about the opposite of being self-centered and list words and phrases that describe that. Finally we connect the word to the book based on what we've read so far and ask ourselves questions trying to connect the book and the word. (See Figure 5.1.)

Students then choose a partner and a word to begin their work. As our class reads the book aloud together, we stop periodically for the partners to discuss their thinking. Then we come back together for partners to share their ideas with the larger group. This helps students who are struggling, by allowing peers to model their thinking instead of me always modeling. This also allows students to piggyback on one another's ideas, even connecting different themes together. This process takes five to ten minutes each day. In its simplicity, this strategy helps students think more deeply about a book that is being read to them—although it works with books they have a copy of as well. Students who choose to reread books now use this strategy to guide their thinking the second time through.

Figure 5.1

Self-Centered

What It Is	What It's Not
being selfish	thoughtful
thinking only of yourself	thinking of others
getting only your way	taking turns
always about you	caring about others
thinking you're the best	nice
sometimes rude	

Connection to the Book . . . So Far

The music teacher is self-centered because he wants to do the concert with the songs he chose and his own way. He doesn't care what the kids think.

Hart is self-centered a little bit. He knows he is cool, and he doesn't think about Mr. Meinert's feelings when he shoots the rubber bands at him. He cares what others think about him.

Questions to Think About

Who is self-centered and how do we know? What might happen if the character(s) stay self-centered? What might happen if the character(s) become selfless and more thoughtful of others? How would these things affect the story?

Student Sample: Katelyn

CONTROL

What it is:

Being in charge

Behaving

Others follow your direction

Telling others what to do

Directing

Having things in order

Managing time

What it's not:

Out of control

Crazy

Loud

Disorganized

Hyper

Flexible

How it relates to the story:

Hart is in control of himself because he does his work and doesn't fool around. He takes the blame for stuff. Hart was out of control when he flung the rubber bands in class and hit his teacher. He didn't mean it—he lost control of the rubber band.

If Hart wasn't in control, he wouldn't be popular, and he'd be a bad student. No one would like him! If he stays in control, he will still be popular and won't be an enemy. He will be appreciated. The trick will be for Hart to control the class, not just himself, and still keep everyone happy.

 **Strategy:** Theme

Purpose: To help students see how a theme of a book is a common thread that runs through the course of the story and that it often helps the reader identify the need for a change in the character and a means to solve the problem of the book.

How: Have some one-word themes already picked out for a book you're reading with your class or a small group. Teach them to keep track of connections to the word and think through the ideas that this word implies. Then show them how to connect the word to the book being read. As students read the book, they work to find examples of this theme developing and how it influences the way the story unfolds.

Writing Connection: When rereading their writer's notebooks to find a pattern, students may realize they have a theme running through their work. Maybe they write about friendships or have several entries that show their love for a favorite pet. Identifying that one-word theme in their own writing, they can then think about what that word means in their life, examples of that word, and examples of opposite meanings. From here, many seeds for writing are planted.

Character Analysis

We were reading the book *Poppy* by Avi (2005). After the first chapter, I stopped to ask my students what they thought of the owl, Mr. Ocax.

"He's mean," said Brandan.

"Yeah, he likes to scare the mice," Ashley agreed.

Students nodded in agreement, and the conversation seemed to stop. So we read on, and I stopped again after a few more chapters. I asked the same question: "What do you think of Mr. Ocax?"

"He's still mean, Ms. B.," Drew explained to me. "He's the enemy."

I smiled. "Enemy sounds much worse than being mean. I can be mean if I'm upset, but I'm not like Mr. Ocax. Let's think about the word *enemy*. Why does it describe Mr. Ocax?"

Emma raised her hand. "He tries to kill the mice and enemies kill people. Like when you're at war."

"Good point. Anyone else?" I asked.

"Enemies tell lies, and Mr. Ocax lies to the mice," Hannah said.

"True," I said, calling on Garrett next.

"Like Emma said—enemies are like at war and they plan attacks. Mr. Ocax thinks through his attacks."

Now that the kids were on a roll, I moved the conversation toward their reader's notebooks. "Wow. When we think of Mr. Ocax as the enemy, our examples seem more specific and even worse than just being mean." Kids nodded, and still some hands waved in the air to give more examples. "Let's hold that conversation for a moment and think: Are there any other words that describe Mr. Ocax well—like *enemy*?" As the kids thought for a moment and talked with their partner, I got out a new piece of chart paper and wrote *Mr. Ocax* at the top. When I turned around, I called their attention back to me, and students began responding:

"Cruel"

"Diabolical"

"Evil"

"Conniving"

"Bully"

"Scary"

I wrote these down as fast as I could and invited students to do the same in their reader's notebooks. "Notice how these words seem more dramatic—more than just mean. Mr. Ocax is mean, but he's more than that, isn't he? Sometimes finding the right word for a character takes some thought.

"We're going to try a strategy in our notebooks to think more deeply about Mr. Ocax. And when you finish, you can try this strategy again with another character from *Poppy* or another book you're reading.

"Choose a word from our list and write it at the top of your page. Then explain how the word describes Mr. Ocax, or another character you're thinking about."

Student Sample: Zoe
Mr. Ocax is SNEAKY

Sneaky people kind of walk up to someone without them knowing they're there. They calculate their plans ahead of time so they don't mess up. for example, Mr. Ocax. He likes to swoop down on his prey without them knowing he's there. Usually good sneaky people are police or detectives. Bad sneaky people are culprites. Mr. Ocax is a bad sneaky.

Notice how Zoe gives some great examples of what a sneaky person would do and how Mr. Ocax is sneaky. She also differentiates between a good sneaky and a bad sneaky. Being able to compare and contrast with the concept of sneaky shows the depth of her understanding.

Student Sample: Garrett
Mr. Ocax is SLY

He tries to be sly by going at night and by creeping up on his prey. Like in the book, he waited for Poppy to come out from under the bark so he could eat her and Ragweed. He swooped down on them when Poppy came out, but only got Ragweed. He scratched Poppy's nose. As it described in the book, Mr. Ocax silently swooped down on the mice. He gets almost perfect with his catches, but not quite. Mr. Ocax is **SLY!** *Late on in the book, he swoops down on Poppy and almost eats her. He missed. He watches from his post to see all of the mice or animals in the forest.*

Garrett tends to repeat himself to try to drive his point home. On the other hand, he gives two clear examples of Mr. Ocax being sly—silently swooping down and watching from his post. Garrett's entry demonstrates understanding of the story and of the character, Mr. Ocax.

This strategy can be extended by continuing conversations with children to make predictions. If Mr. Ocax is sneaky, then what do you think he'll do next? If Mr. Ocax is a liar, are there any characters you can trust? Eventually, as students are engaged in this rich conversation coupled with this strategy, you can nudge their thinking in their notebooks to include forming some of these questions and making predictions about a character's motives throughout the book. Students then practice this strategy on characters from their own books that they have chosen to read.

Student Sample: Emma
Granny Relda is SURPRISING
(Based on The Fairy-Tale Detectives)

She isn't a normal grandma. Well, the girls don't know if she's really her grandma or not. So that is a surprise right there. Even if she is the grandma, she definitely has some tricks up her sleeve. She has magical spells on her house. She has a locked door to a room no one is allowed to enter. Her dog is HUGE and she makes odd colored spaghetti! Then, if that's not enough, she thinks of herself as a detective. A grandma as a detective. She must be smart and nosey. Detectives have to ask a lot of questions. I think the girls can trust her.

Here Emma takes a character from her own reading to try this strategy. As a reader, she seems surprised by this character and is having a hard time trying to figure her out. In the end, Emma trusts this character, but my guess is, she keeps a close eye on Granny Relda.

Character Connections

I was at a writing conference in the North Georgia mountains. Esteemed writers like Lola Schaefer, April Pulley Sayre, and Rebecca Dotlich were there. I was going from session to session to learn how to write for children. Many people would say, How hard can that really be? You come up with an idea, you write about it, revise it, send it out, hope for the best, and *poof!* like magic you have a book. Besides, only the lucky ones get published, right? *Wrong.*

The complex nature behind even the easy readers was unveiled to us. The patterns of text, the planning, the "beginner's mistakes," and the depth of the authors' knowledge about literature in general was nothing but inspiring. I left not wanting to write books for children but wanting to go back to college to learn more about writing.

I began using some of their ideas with my fourth graders immediately, one of which was connecting characters. As good readers figure out, an author never inserts a character into a story without a reason. There are no extras. In addition, all of the characters are somehow connected—through motive, relation, or even conflict. Editors expect this connection, and they often throw out any extras that don't meet this expectation. It is also an important thing for readers to know. Because, now, we have another way to look beyond the words to see the story unfold from the inside out. April Pulley Sayre taught me this, and for that I'm forever grateful.

After learning something new, like the way characters connect within a story, I usually start introducing the concept to my class with a book I know well. In October, that means pulling out *Goblins in the Castle* (Coville 1992). I should note that I read several books with my class that are my favorites and that I consider classics. *Goblins* is one of those books. However, between these favorites, I expose my students to many different genres and newer stories to keep up with the ever-growing market of children's literature.

Character Connections: The Lesson

William is the main character, and I write his name in the middle of a piece of chart paper. I then draw an arrow and write the name Igor, another character.

"How would you describe the connection between William and Igor?" I ask my class.

"Igor is William's friend," says Dean.

I write *friend* near the arrow.

"Igor lives in the dungeon of the castle where William lives," adds Alon.

I write *lives in dungeon in castle with William.* "What else?" I ask.

"Igor seems to trust William, and he's the only one William has to talk to," Emma says.

I pause and ask, "Do you think William trusts Igor?"

"Yes," says Emma.

So I write *trust each other* and *talk to each other.*

"I think they're both lonely. Is that a connection?" asks Zoe.

"Yes," I agree and write *lonely* near the arrow.

"I know!" Dean interjects, with his eyes wide, indicating a really good idea. "Igor guarded the goblins in the castle and William lets the goblins out. They both have something to do with the goblins."

"Interesting observation, Dean." After adding Dean's comments, I continue, "We have a good list here of how these two characters connect. You see, it turns out that authors . . ."

". . . only use characters that have something to do with the story. The character always comes back," Drew parrots to me.

"Yes, I'm glad you listen. But I was going to say that all of the characters in the book are somehow connected. It's like a huge plate of spaghetti where all the noodles are going one way or another. They twist and turn into a big heap on your plate. And even though each noodle is one piece, it touches and connects with the others on your plate. It's kind of like that with characters in the story. They all connect to each other—one way or another."

We continue to look at the character connections to William, and we add to our chart as new characters are introduced. (See Figure 5.2.)

Figure 5.2

Character Connections in *Goblins in the Castle*

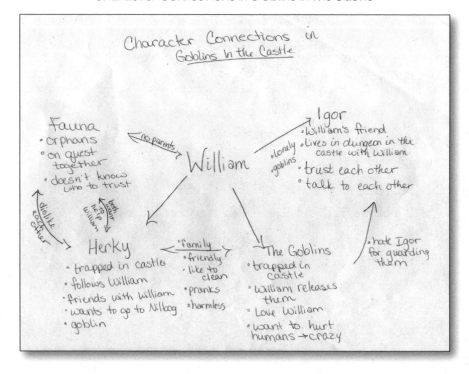

This work with connections was all very interesting and kept the children thinking about the characters and how they work together in a story. Although I didn't require it this time around, many children started keeping their own web of characters in their notebooks. Some even started keeping character connections for their independent reading books. "It helps me keep track of who's who," Emma told me in a reading conference one day.

Strategy: Character Connections

Purpose: To recognize how characters within a book are connected to each other. It helps the reader unveil the characters' motives as well as make better predictions and inferences regarding the characters and plot development.

How: Model these kinds of connections with a read-aloud or story the whole class is reading. This can be done with a picture book or a novel. Show students how to make a web with the characters on a piece of chart paper. Then ask the children to work in pairs or individually to do the same for the book they are reading. This can also be done in a guided reading group.

Writing Connection: When students write, I often find they have too many characters to handle. They want all of their friends to be in their next adventure. As a prewriting or revision strategy, children can plan their characters with this same format. Each character needs to have a connection that is important to the story. If it's just that the characters are friends and there is no other connection, then that character should be saved for another time.

Lifting a Prompt

Back in Chapter 1, I wrote about the experience I had with my class after reading *Harvesting Hope* by Kathleen Krull. That memory haunts me as I try to figure out how to bridge the class conversation to individual notebooks. In my personal adult book groups, I often leave our discussions thinking about what people said and writing about how the conversation pushed my thinking about the book. Children don't do this naturally, and I have spent many years trying to figure out how to do this without giving them a prompt that a publisher or I came up with from the book. I wanted to push students' thinking in a way that was directly impacted by the conversations generated in class. And as any good teacher knows, you just can't plan what kids will say.

I'm really fascinated by the concept of character connections in the light that April shined on it for me. It is interesting to see how the characters connect in a book in this way, because, for me, it helps reveal how the author creates conflict, tension, and suspense in the story. It keeps kids on the lookout for new characters and their place in the bigger picture instead of focusing on the chapter or page at hand. But there is more. I am convinced that understanding character connections helps children make better predictions, infer more deeply and often, and gain a better grasp of the overall story.

Lifting a Prompt: The Lesson

We had just read the part of the book in *Goblins in the Castle* where the goblins have been released from the castle and a little goblin named Herky has joined William on his quest to save Igor and stop the goblin war against humans. On our character-connection chart, we added goblins and Herky, but as we talked about these connections, I didn't add them to the chart this time. I wanted to lead the conversation further—beyond the chart. I was going to lift a prompt from our conversation.

This is generally a teacher-directed (reader's-guide) strategy that leads students to the notebook. I've wrestled with the idea of prompts, but realized that many times my students have responded in their notebooks regarding our conversation about a book. Thereby the prompt is organic by nature—it comes naturally from our thinking as a class.

I do have to prepare for this, although sometimes it just happens. In general, in order to lift a prompt from a conversation, there first needs to be a conversation among the children. This means I'm not asking questions and looking for specific answers. We're talking about our thinking during our reading of the book. As I teach comprehension strategies and the children become used to thinking while they read and to recognizing that thinking, the conversations initiated and generated by the students become easier and more natural. There comes a point when I can literally start a class conversation about a book by saying, "So, tell me what you're thinking." And they do.

Second, as the conversation unfolds, I have to listen carefully and ask questions to clarify or push the thinking further. It's important that all of the children are engaged as much as possible, because it's from here that we'll get fodder for our thinking in our notebooks. Eventually, my goal is for students to simply respond to our conversations as naturally as I would after a book-group conversation. In the beginning, they need more help than that.

Third, I keep notes on chart paper. I'm modeling what good listeners do when they want to remember what is being said or what they want to think more about later. Some children will naturally take out their notebooks and begin copying what I write; some will just watch and listen. Either way, the modeling is important so they can see my thinking and how I arrive at what to put in my notebook later. (See Figure 5.3 for an example of my notes from *Goblins in the Castle*.)

Figure 5.3

William–Herky–and the Goblins
Thinking Beyond the Connections

Is Herky a spy? Can he be trusted? He's a goblin—may really be on the goblins' side. How do you know?

The goblins are mad but are they bad? The things in the castle were pranks but didn't hurt anyone. If they can turn furniture upside down and hang it from the ceiling, they could have hurt someone. Strong.

And clean—the whole castle was clean in a night. What's NILBOG?

The goblins took Igor—William's friend. If Igor is good, then the goblins must be bad.

The goblins didn't take William. Why not? Do the goblins like him? Why?

The goblins should be nice to William, because he let them out. They hate Igor for keeping them in. (Connection from our earlier character chart!)

The next day, after going through this process with my students and thinking about the notes I took in class and what we have read in the book, I was ready to lift the prompt and ask the kids to write about their thinking in their reader's notebooks. I gave them the chart shown in Figure 5.4 to glue into their notebooks and respond to.

Figure 5.4

Goblins in the Castle
by Bruce Coville

Begin rethinking the connections each of these characters has with William.

Igor	
Herky	
Goblins	

We are at a point in the story where the goblins have captured Igor. William is told that the goblins are good but angry at all the humans for being locked up so long. William is befriended by the goblins as their hero but all the other humans in the world must die. And Igor finds out William let the goblins out of the castle. *What a mess!*

How do you think the relationships above will help or hurt William in his quest to stop the goblin war? Use what you know about the story, examples in the book, your thinking about character connections, and notes from our conversations to help you reflect and respond.

This prompt may seem like a typical prompt that could have been written before the novel began. And that's true, it could have, but it wouldn't have worked as well. I was able to pull the character connections into a chart to help start student thinking. I gave a quick summary of where we left off in the story so the kids won't have to worry about that in their writing. (It drives me crazy when kids spend a whole page on retelling the story I just read with them before they start in on their own thinking.) The question, however, relates to the notes from our conversation the day before. Is Herky a spy? Can he be trusted to help William, or will he deliver William into a goblin trap? Are the goblins bad or just mad—what will they do to William if they find out he intends to stop the war? And what about Igor? He's William's friend but is hated by the goblins. Will William stand up for his friend and risk his safety with the goblins? All of this is rolled into the question, How do you think the relationships above will help or hurt William in his quest to stop the goblin war?

I could have given this as a cold prompt to see what the kids thought. But, really, how many nine-year-olds can infer and write a thoughtful response to this without any help? Because the prompt came from a conversation, I knew my students were already thinking about these relationships and how they were impacting the story. This was the nudge to move their thinking from their own thoughts, to mix those thoughts with the conversation we had, and then to grow a new understanding of the story and its characters. That's pretty intense for fourth grade, but it works at other grade levels too.

I guess the difference is this—a typical, planned prompt is going to happen regardless of the conversations you and your class have about a book. A prompt you lift from conversation happens because of what your students have said about the book.

Student Sample: Jessica
Character Connections for
Goblins in the Castle

Figure 5.5

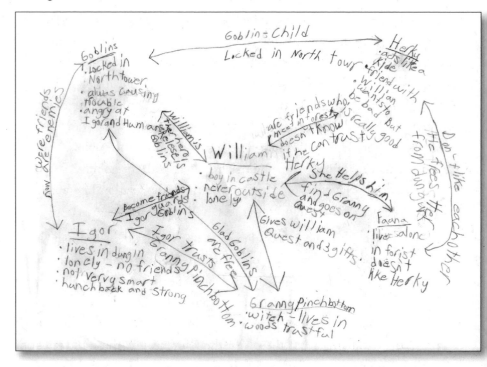

Response: I think Herky might be able to create some cover for William. Since the goblins trust Herky, because he is one of them, he could distract them long enough for William to fasten the collar around the goblin king's neck.

I don't think the relationship between William and the goblins would give the goblins any benefits. William has nothing to offer the goblins, except maybe Herky, which would not be fair to Herky. The goblins will be able to use their mystical powers that Granny Pinchbottom told William about to hurt William or Igor. The goblins might be mean to William and not want to free Igor.

This is showing me a lot about Jessica's understanding of the book we're reading. She definitely has the right ideas on her chart (Figure 5.5), but when she goes to write about her thoughts, she forgets about the chart. Jessica says there is no benefit to the goblin's relationship with William in her writing, but in the chart she says that William let the goblins out. That's an important detail that Jessica knows but hasn't really integrated into her thinking yet. If she just filled out a worksheet or just wrote a response, this gap wouldn't be evident. Now with a conference or a small-group discussion, I can help fill that gap in her reading and teach her to look for those gaps when she reads other books.

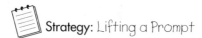 **Strategy:** Lifting a Prompt

Purpose: To guide student response to a book or conversation about reading. Using the conversation with students as fodder for thought, the teacher—or, eventually, the students—pushes their thinking with a prompt that grows out of the conversation itself.

How: First, initiate a conversation with the students regarding a book the class or group is reading together. Second, take notes about what the students say, including questions they may have, inferences, connections, and so on. Third, think about what they said and how, as the "reader's guide," you can push their thinking further. Create an open-ended question that connects to the conversation and yet leads the students to further thinking and reflection.

Writing Connection: The idea behind lifting a prompt is to eventually lead students to prompt—ignite or push—their own thinking. I found using news magazines like *Time for Kids*, *National Geographic Explorer*, and *Scholastic News* lend themselves to kids prompting their own thinking. Reading a news magazine article may lead students to ask themselves questions such as What do I think about this? What connection does this have for me? What else do I want to know? If the students' thoughts on the topic are ignited, it will help them develop seed ideas for future research, reading, and writing.

Chapter 6
Assessment: A Tool for Teaching in the Now

The first day back from summer break, our school has a long faculty meeting. At the beginning of the meeting we get the school calendar. Almost immediately, I notice teachers stop listening and start counting. Some are counting the number of days until the first school holiday. Others are counting and dividing up their lesson-plan books into chunks for units of study. And some are counting the number of days of mandatory testing.

As I travel around the country, I find that every teacher has a horror story about how much they test and how much time it takes away from instruction. Knowing ahead of time that my students will be tested at the whim of a politician, I—like many teachers—have started to reassess the amount of testing I do in my classroom. And I've noticed teachers have moved from giving "tests" to giving "assessments." Somehow changing the word makes it more palatable, but it's not only that. Although some people use the words interchangeably, there is a difference between the two.

When we test, we assess what children know based on a onetime performance on a set of predetermined questions or prompts based on curriculum objectives. Oftentimes we test at the end of a unit of study, semester, or school year. The results inform teaching—but in reality they don't change our teaching until the following school year when we teach the material again.

When I assess children in my classroom, it's based on their performance over a period of time. I use a preponderance of evidence to determine their progress. This information, which is gathered on an ongoing basis, guides my teaching in the *now*. It shows me where kids are at present, where they were a few days or weeks ago, and what I need to do next to push them forward.

There is a place for testing within school. But it should not be confused with ongoing assessment of student work. When I assess the reader's notebook, it's not like giving a paper and pencil test to assess comprehension. I'm looking over several entries—gathering evidence—to note each reader's strengths and weaknesses. In order to do this, it is necessary to identify what I try to accomplish with the reader's notebook. (See Figure 6.1.) I've found it's important for me to be clear in my own mind about what I'm trying to accomplish, how I'm going to accomplish it, and how I'm going to assess it before I hold students accountable for things. That's not to say that I haven't learned by trial and error, because I have—more times than I care to count. But I find I am more purposeful and intentional with my teaching and planning when I have an idea of what I'm aiming for.

When I look at my list of the various things I try to accomplish, I'm always amazed at how much I can get done with this one notebook. However, it's not the end-all and be-all of teaching reading. Reading and thinking is far more complex than a few comprehension and notebook strategies. To fully assess a reader, we must take in a variety of assessments and funnel them into a grade for a report card. I am fortunate to work for a school system that still allows for teacher decision making in this realm. I determine what contributes to my students' report card grades.

Determining a grade—one grade—for a variety of processes that are a part of reading and comprehending is no small task. It's why we teachers fret about it at the end of each instructional session. Did we grade the right things? Does this accurately reflect the student's performance and progress? Is this a truthful snapshot of what I see happening in the classroom? It's a daunting task, but one that I welcome. Having thought out ahead of time how I'll assess student work helps me monitor student progress.

Figure 6.1

Determining Purpose for a Reader's Notebook

Questions to Ask Yourself	My Personal Responses (curriculum responses based on Gwinnett County Public Schools Academic Knowledge and Skills)
1. What *reading* curriculum objectives am I trying to accomplish using the reader's notebook as a tool?	*Identify characters, plot, setting* *Demonstrate efficiency in predicting, summarizing, and inferring* *Identify theme and interpret metaphors and similes* *Analyze characters and their actions* *Compare and contrast*
2. What *writing* curriculum objectives will the reader's notebook support?	*Write a response to literature that is interpretative, evaluative, or reflective* *Write essays that are three or more paragraphs* *Edit writing for spelling, grammar, and usage* *Use figurative or novel language*
3. How often will students write in their reader's notebook?	*Two to three times a week* *At least once a week at home to demonstrate independence*
4. What will students be responsible for having in their reader's notebook?	*Writing that shows an attempt at using the strategies I demonstrate* *Evidence that they are using the strategies with a variety of books* *Notes from mini-lessons regarding comprehension strategies, guided reading groups, literature circles* *Thoughtful responses* *Evidence that demonstrates independence by selecting and using notebook strategies for thinking about books they choose to read independently*

Yet assessing kids needs to be somewhat flexible as we learn and adjust to student needs. It's just like teaching a well-planned lesson. No matter how much planning and preparation I do, there is always the chance that a student will say, think, or do something that will change the course of the lesson—ideally for the better. It's the same way with assessment. Sometimes I'll read students' notebooks or confer with them and they are doing much greater things than my assessment tool notes. Or they'll take a strategy and use it differently than I had intended, but it makes so much sense the way they used it. Where does that come in to my assessment if it wasn't on my preplanned list of criteria? I found I need to be responsive and try to keep up with my students. Involving students in assessment is key for me. Using a variety of assessment tools helps me develop a better understanding of each child's progress.

Self-Evaluations

Helping children to develop an intrinsic sense of accomplishment is important; it allows them to move from the constant need for teacher approval to having confidence in one's own ability. I had a college professor who had us turn in our papers by the grade we expected to get. First he'd dismiss all of the students who expected As, and they'd turn in their papers as they left. Then he'd dismiss the Bs, Cs, Ds, and finally the Fs. My friend was still seated after the students with F papers were dismissed. The professor addressed her and the few others who were still there. He gave them a slip of paper with this written on it: "If it is to be, it is up to me."

He explained that if they were to be successful in life, they had better learn to determine what their best work is or what the best level of work they are willing to do is. From there, they needed to learn how to compare their work with external expectations. In this case, it's a college professor; in other cases it may be a boss, a neighbor, or even a spouse. The professor told them that they needed to develop this sense in order to be successful in life, and when my friend asked how to do this, he said by trial and error.

I think about this story a lot. I used to get frustrated with my mom, who would answer my "Is it good?" question with another question that would make me think about whether or not it would be considered good. She wasn't being mean, but, rather, she was teaching me to exercise and develop the skill of self-evaluation. Sometimes I was right and sometimes I wasn't. But through trial and error, I've learned how to know when I have done my best work.

Intrinsic evaluation is difficult for children, but we can help develop that sense with guiding questions and opportunities for children to evaluate their own work and thinking processes. The point isn't necessarily to put a grade in my grade book, but rather to get an inside look at my students' viewpoint on how the work is going. Oftentimes this brings to light misunderstandings and frustrations children are dealing with but haven't been able to express. It's a key technique in gathering a preponderance of evidence of how students are doing in my class.

Self-evaluations take four forms in my class right now: guiding questions, free responses, rubrics, and portfolio development. Guiding questions, free responses, and rubrics all connect directly to the reader's notebook. All three processes require students to reread past entries and reflect on their progress as readers. Portfolio development, although another part of my assessment plan, involves much more than the reader's notebook—here we look at book lists, running records, literature circle work, technology projects, and multigenre projects. Some of this is predetermined by my school, and other aspects are determined by each individual student. I'll keep my discussion of self-evaluations focused on the three forms that primarily involve the reader's notebook.

I do not use all of these forms of self-evaluation all of the time, nor at the same time. I use them at different times of the year and with different kids. The reality is you just can't do everything all of the time with every child in every school year. It's important to have several assessment tools to choose from, however, so that you can make informed choices about how you'll assess, when you'll assess, and for what reason.

Guiding Questions

After a couple of weeks of keeping reader's notebooks, I gather the students together to talk about them.

"Today we're going to talk about keeping a reader's notebook. You've been working in your notebook for a couple of weeks now. What do you think of it?" I want to keep the question open-ended so I can get honest feedback.

Emma raises her hand immediately. "It's very difficult. I haven't had to do this before. I'm not sure it's always right."

"When things are new to me, they can be difficult. I understand what you mean, Emma. Do you think you're getting the hang of it though?"

She nods slowly. "I think so. But just when I think I get it, you give us a new strategy."

I nod, noting that I may need to slow down introducing new strategies. "What else do you think?" I ask the rest of the class. Sensing relief from the other students regarding my reaction to Emma's honest answer, more hands go up.

"I like it better than workbook pages," Trey begins, "but sometimes I worry I don't write enough."

"It helps me. I'm thinking about things differently than I did last year. The strategies help me fill the page," says another child.

The responses keep coming, and they are different from child to child. Finally, I stop this part of the conversation to lead them into the guided questions.

"I think you all have been doing a terrific job trying the strategies and working in your notebook. I like to think of the reader's notebook like a sister or brother to the writer's notebook. They're similar but totally different."

"Yeah," says Emma. "They both have strategies and your thinking, but one is based on a book and the other is based on your life."

"Exactly. Think back to when you first kept a writer's notebook. It was a little scary, filling those empty pages with nothing but your life to go on. But you got the hang of it, and the reader's notebook will come along that way too. Today, I'm going to ask you to reread and think about your work in your notebook. You'll write an entry to tell me about your progress."

With big eyes and an expression of fear, Dean shouts out, "How am I going to do *that*!"

"Don't worry. Today I have some questions you can use to guide your thinking and your response. If you find yourself wanting to write more than what the questions ask for, you may. Use the questions to get yourself started."

Developing questions for this kind of assessment takes some planning. I consider the time of year or how long we've been keeping notebooks. I think about my notebook rubric and the criteria I've established for my students. I think about the comprehension strategies and notebook strategies the children know or have been practicing. Because all of this changes as the year goes on, the guiding questions change as well. In general, I ask myself some guiding questions that help me determine what kinds of questions to ask for student reflection. (See Figure 6.2 for a look at how I come up with guiding questions. A blank copy of the form used in Figure 6.2 is located in the appendix. Figure 6.3 is a list of the final questions that I give this particular class.)

Because the students have done self-evaluations on their writer's notebooks, they know they will need to reread their entries before responding to any of the questions. I also remind them that they can use examples from their notebooks to support their assessment. Then I assure them that there are no wrong answers. This is a time for them to think like a teacher in the sense that they're evaluating themselves, so they can then see what areas they need to focus on and what areas they're doing really well with.

Figure 6.2

Teacher Form: Guiding Questions

Category of Thinking	Questions I Ask Myself and Possible Answers	Possible Guiding Questions for Students
Student as a Reader	**What kind of reading behaviors have we talked about lately?** Students have reflected on their history as a reader. We have worked with plot structure.	What is one thing you want to improve about your reading? How does knowing plot structure help you anticipate what happens in your story?
Comprehension Strategies	**What strategies have we been focusing on in mini-lessons?** We've been discussing the three levels of visualization.	What kind of visualizing do you find yourself doing most? How does this help you understand the story? What gets in your way of "being in" the story?
Notebook Strategies	**Which notebook strategies have I introduced and which ones have the students have been practicing?** Introduced Leaning In and the Fab Five. Practiced History of a Reader and What I Know to Be True About Reading.	We have used and practiced four strategies lately. Which one has been the most helpful for your thinking about reading? Which one is still confusing or not helpful to you? Explain to help me understand your opinion.
Effort	**What qualities are the students aware of that demonstrate their effort?** We have compared thoughtful and rote entries. We've discussed the importance of practicing good writing habits.	As you reread your entries, have you put forth your best effort? Do your entries sound like the thinking in your mind? Have you practiced good writing habits, including spelling and punctuation?

Figure 6.3

Guiding Questions for Self-Evaluation

1. What is one thing you want to improve about your reading?

2. What kind of visualizing do you find yourself doing most? How does this help you understand the story? What gets in your way of "being in" the story?

3. We have used and practiced four strategies lately. Which one has been the most helpful for your thinking about reading? Which one is still confusing or not helpful to you? Explain to help me understand your opinion.

4. As you reread your entries, have you put forth your best effort? Do your entries sound like the thinking in your mind? Have you practiced good writing habits, including spelling and punctuation?

5. If you had to give yourself a grade on your work so far, what would it be? Use the notebook rubric to help you. Give at least two reasons why you deserve this grade.

Questions I Ask Myself—and Possible Answers

When I approach my class with the idea of self-evaluations, students often think that this will be a piece of cake. The crooked grins that cross their faces lead me to believe that, at first, students see this as an easy A. So I find it necessary to approach this topic with an air of importance and not just as another day of writing in our reader's notebooks. For this reason, I'm very explicit when I give them directions—so much so that the children will need a copy of the self-evaluation questions to help keep them on track. Very quickly, students realize that when I'm setting them up for self-evaluations, it's going to take some time, thought, and effort on their part.

Depending on the makeup of my class, I've found that how I disperse the guiding questions actually makes a difference. Sometimes I'm able to pull the questions I generate on the teacher form and retype them in paragraph form (Figure 6.3). Students can then paste the questions into their notebooks and answer each question (or set of questions) in numerical order. Other times, I align the questions with the different categories of thinking I used for the teacher form (Figures 6.2 and 6.4). Students can also paste these questions into their notebooks and respond to them on subsequent notebook pages. This format allows both me and the students some flexibility. Because the questions are not numbered, students may choose to answer one or all of the questions in each category. In addition, students can use each category of thinking as a main idea for a paragraph, thereby responding in paragraph form rather than a numerical sequence.

I find that I tend to use the list of questions more in the beginning of the year, when students are still getting used to the idea of the notebooks and self-evaluations. As students become better writers and less inhibited with regard to writing about their thinking, I want to give them more flexibility while still giving them some guidance. Using the categories with some guiding questions seems to offer that flexibility, even if the questions are essentially the same.

Figure 6.4

Student Form: Guiding Questions

Category of Thinking	Guiding Questions for Students
Student as a Reader	How has learning about rising action and climax helped you understand your book(s) better? What is one thing you want to improve about your reading?
Comprehension Strategies	What kind of visualizing do you find yourself doing most? How does this help you understand the story? What gets in your way of "being in" the story?
Notebook Strategies	We have used and practiced four strategies lately. Which one has been the most helpful for your thinking about reading? Which one is still confusing or not helpful to you? Explain to help me understand your opinion.
Effort	As you reread your entries, have you put forth your best effort? Do your entries sound like the thinking in your mind? Have you practiced good writing habits that include attention to punctuation and spelling?

Depending on your class, you may not want to use all four categories for self-reflection. Many students may feel overwhelmed and defeated before even starting. If that's the case, it's fine to wade into this form of assessment by asking students to respond to just one category. I have done this both ways based on what I think my students can handle. When I start with one category, I gradually add on a new one each time we use this evaluation method, which is usually once every four to six weeks.

Student Sample: Self-Evaluation by Emma

1. *I'm a great reader. I read very fast, and sometimes I skip boring parts, like when the writer goes on and on about the scenery. I don't always like that. I think I need to slow down a little bit, but I don't know how. I just go fast. Do I need harder books?*

2. *If it's a good book I am usually IN THE STORY! If it's not a book I'm interested in, I have to really force myself to see things. Then it's more like a movie. I don't mind that, but it's not as cool as feeling like I'm there. When I read social studies and science stuff, I don't visualize. Should I?*

3. *Leaning In makes me slow down. I don't really like it, but it forces me to reread and think about one part. I guess that's good.*

4. *YES! YES!*

5. *Definitely an A. I write every time you tell us to write and try the strategies.*

· ❋ · ❋ · ❋ ·

Student Sample: Self-Evaluation by Dean

1. *I don't really like to read, except war books. I want to find a book I like.*

2. *I see the still pictures. When Ms. B. reads to us, I see pictures like in a picture book. Sometimes, if I'm reading an easy book, I can see the movie. I've never been IN the book. I'm not sure what that means.*

3. *The Fab Five helps me write the right number of sentences before I stop. I'm still confused about being IN the book.*

4. *I guess I can try harder. I have a hard time writing about my thinking when I'm thinking about the book. That's why I like the Fab Five.*

5. *I think I should get an A. I'm writing about my thinking, I just don't have a lot to say.*

· ❋ · ❋ · ❋ ·

Student Sample: Self-Evaluation by Katelyn

I'm a very good reading student. I like to read books. I think it's interesting that learning about plot structure, a.k.a. rising action and climax, has helped me be better at predicting. For example, I know in Peter and the Star Catchers, *the first time Peter tries to keep the star dust won't succeed. It's too early in the book. So I start to think about the different things he'll have to overcome. Then I notice one thing leads to another—he lands on an island near where the star dust has drifted ashore. BUT he's taken prisoner by the tribe. Then he makes friends with the tribe and goes to find the star stuff. BUT the pirates arrive. You see what I mean. So really, I'm reading to figure out how Peter is going to get the star stuff and beat the pirates once and for all. (That will be the climax. Right?)*

I'm also a good reading student because I visualize all of my books. I feel like I'm IN books mostly when they're realistic. With Peter and the Star Catchers *it's like I'm watching a movie. I think it's because I know it really can't happen. It's entertaining, but not very realistic. So even though I don't get IN every book, I know I'm still using other parts of the visualizing strategy.*

I am also a good reading student because I put forth my best effort when writing in here. I think my responses sound like me and give you a peek inside my head. I think a lot when I read, which means I'm comprehending. I'm also a good speller and use ending punctuation.

Notice how the structure of the student responses relates to how the guiding questions are presented. Both Emma and Dean number their responses, answering the questions. Katelyn, however, responds in paragraphs and gives more information to develop her main ideas. Again, a lot of this has to do with the time of year and the abilities of individual students. With either setup, I'm getting a lot of valuable information.

It's interesting to note that, although Emma's and Dean's responses are so different, they both arrive at the same overall grade of an A. However, just from reading the two samples, most teachers can make a decision about who the better reader—or A student—may be. Through both of these samples, one can glean a lot of useful information.

Emma is clearly confident about her reading. She is comfortable with the kinds of books she chooses, and she's aware of how her thinking changes depending on what she reads. It's interesting that she asks questions in her evaluation, giving herself more to think about or at least an opening for me to confer with her. Overall, Emma is a typical A student, but sometimes helping these readers see that there are ways to improve is hard to do. This assessment—with Emma's own questions in the responses—opens doors for me to teach her about extending comprehension strategies to all subject areas and how to slow down her reading.

Dean seems less confident or at least like he doesn't care to read. He likes to do the minimum of what is required, as evidenced by his misunderstanding the purpose of the Fab Five strategy. Yet he also recognizes that when the books he reads are easier, his visualization is stronger. This clues me in to the fact that he may be reading books that are too difficult for him, even if he's able to call out the words. It's also a start for him to self-evaluate more appropriately. "Easy" books really may be "just right" for him. Helping him adjust this measure of just-right books will increase his ability to self-evaluate the kinds of books he chooses. In addition, it will help him in his response to books; the ones he understands will allow him to think about his reading and the meaning of the text, rather than struggling to make a picture in his mind.

Katelyn's response seems very sophisticated in relation to the others. She isn't necessarily a stronger reader than the others, but by developing paragraphs, she is able to put more details into her response.

Notice how she uses the thinking categories as part of her topic sentences. I think Katelyn's first paragraph is interesting, because she almost slips into a summary of the book she's reading. She is able to relate these events to the idea of rising action in a book, which helps me understand how well she is applying what she is learning. At the end of that paragraph, she is still questioning what the climax will be for the book she's reading. But it also leads me to believe that she doesn't understand what the climax of the story is well enough to determine when it occurs in a story. It's a complicated skill, and I can see where she'll need some support.

As Katelyn goes on in her response, I learn a lot about how her ability to visualize correlates to the kind of book she is reading—realistic fiction or fantasy. It makes me wonder how she uses this strategy with historical fiction and nonfiction. Both are realistic and can, or did, happen. So, will she be able to be IN the book with these genres? This question will give Katelyn a purpose for exploring different genres in her reading.

All three student samples come from capable readers. They scored similarly on different standardized and nonstandardized reading tests. The differences in their responses, however, give me a different kind of insight into each one as an individual reader. In turn, I can offer timely support and enrichment.

Free Response

As I get busy during the school year, I often forget to stop and reflect on my teaching. I try to take one or two Saturday mornings a month to go into my classroom when I can be alone and it's quiet. It gives me time to review what my class has done, what my class is currently working on, and where my class needs to go. From here, I begin, revise, or edit lesson plans based on my students' needs. This is how I get the reflection time into my life. It works for me.

My students are busy too. From their point of view, their whole school day is filled with work, and when they get home they have places to go. So it's hard for them to understand how to carve out time for reflection. My friend and former colleague Judy Eggemeier used to say, "If it's important enough to do well, it's important enough to do at school." I know we all have packed curriculums that take more than the hours the school day allows. Yet, because I think this form of assessment is important, I give students time during the school day to look at their work, past and present, and think about their own progress. This can be done with guiding questions, but there are times I just want kids to choose what they want to say about their progress—to focus on what they want to focus on.

Student Sample: Ashley

I'm still writing a lot of summaries. At least I'm not retelling everything. I am trying to dig deeper, like when we talk in our class. It's hard for me, because I'm so focused on each part of the story, I forget to look deeper.

· ✳ · ✳ · ✳ ·

Student Sample: Roasia

When I don't get something, I reread it and then I understood it. When I read the titles I know what it's mostly going to be about. If I don't know what a book or article is about, it can be boring. I ask myself questions to keep me thinking so I don't get confused.

· ✳ · ✳ · ✳ ·

Student Sample: Alan

I love my notebook. I can revisit my thinking about books. I like writing in my notebook after we talk—like in our literature group. It helps me think more clearly. I hope that's not cheating. I'm good at the questioning strategy and visualizing. I draw good pictures.

Rubrics

When I was growing up, my mom was a teacher at my school. Whenever I had a project to do, I wanted her to grade it before I turned it in. I needed an official opinion to see if I had a chance at getting the A. My mom started to teach me to think like a teacher. She taught me to ask myself questions: Does my project show I understood its purpose? Did I address all of the directions? Did I include examples or illustrations? Did I edit my work? Did I do my best? If I could answer yes to all of these questions, I had a shot at getting a good grade.

Rubrics have erased that kind of guesswork for the students. A well-written rubric can be a useful tool for students, teachers, and parents. Teachers, school systems, and publishers alike have gotten on this band-wagon, and one can find a rubric for just about anything. Online, I found rubrics from brushing your teeth like an expert to keeping a clean desk. Making expectations clear is the cornerstone of using a rubric.

For reader's notebooks, it's important to think about the objectives and purpose of the notebook when considering a rubric. Jennifer Moon, a third-grade teacher at my school, allocates a point system to score her students' reading responses. What I find particularly interesting is how she includes an interpretation of the criteria being evaluated. (See Figure 6.5.)

Using a rubric with an interpretation guide helps Jennifer communicate not only with her students but with the parents as well. I've been on the wrong side of the conference table having to explain a grade or how I assessed a certain project. It's important to have the expectations thought out ahead of time, align them with curriculum objectives, and communicate them to both students and parents before misunderstandings occur.

Jennifer's rubric is for each entry. When I collect the reader's notebooks, it's to gather a preponderance of evidence. I'm looking across several entries to glean insight to student thinking and progress. Because of the way the notebook is set up, kids may be writing in it more than once a week and the entries may be of different lengths. Therefore, for me, I've turned to a rubric more like the one I use for writer's notebooks (Buckner 2005).

Figure 6.5

Jennifer Moon's Reading Response Rubric

Rubric for Reading Response	Excellent	Good	Attempting	No Attempt
Capturing Your Thinking I talked about at least three different ideas I had about the book, and I showed my thinking by using some of these strategies: 1. Discussing my thinking about the story (Characters, Setting, Plot, Solution, Theme, etc.) 2. Connecting—showing evidence from the book 3. Predicting/Inferring 4. Questioning 5. Reacting to what is happening in the story I answered the questions my teacher asked me from my last letter in complete sentences.	4	3	2	1
Thoughtfulness/Details I supported my thoughts with evidence from the text. I explained my thinking with telling why I think what I do (because . . .). I showed that I understand my job as a reader and a writer for my response. I put effort into my letter with meaningful thinking and/or questioning about the book I am responding to.	4	3	2	1
Clarity I wrote a response that makes sense. It was easy for the reader to understand my thinking. I showed the ability to express my thinking clearly with complete sentences.	4	3	2	1

Figure 6.5 (continued)

Rubric for Reading Response	Excellent	Good	Attempting	No Attempt
Voice/Personality My response is interesting to read, not just a boring list of ideas. It has comments about my thinking (What would I do? How would I feel?).	4	3	2	1
Grammar, Usage, Mechanics, and Spelling (GUMS), Timeliness, and Neatness My response was edited for proper grammar and spelling. It was turned in on time and written neatly. I had all the parts of a letter. I wrote a new paragraph for each new thought/idea.	4	3	2	1

Teacher Evaluations: A Rubric for the Reader's Notebook

I'm wordy. I love to play Scrabble and Text Twist. I love to read aloud just for the sound of it. I even love teaching vocabulary to students. And to tell the truth, I've always gotten a kick out of running the word-count function when writing on the computer. So when it comes time to create a rubric—where few words are used—it gets complicated. Some teachers I know can just whip up a rubric like a grocery list. I'm a bit slower in developing rubrics, because I want just one rubric for the notebook as a whole, not one for each entry or strategy. Nonetheless, the rubrics I provide in this book are things I use in my classroom. I encourage teachers to use them as a starting point and to adapt the wording and criteria to fit their own curriculum needs.

I try to keep the rubric simple and to the point. Since it will be used to assess several entries at once, I don't want to get too bogged down in the details. If I want to grade just one entry, I'd use a rubric more like Jennifer Moon's. I also have adjusted the rubric to have grades rather than labels for excellent, good, fair, and unacceptable work. I do this mainly because kids and parents make the switch anyway. In their minds excellent = A, good = B, and so on. In addition, the fact of the matter is that I still need to transfer the information to a grade for my grade book. That transfer shouldn't be a secret. I don't want parents surprised by grades on the report card, and I believe I have the responsibility to help parents understand where and how grades are gathered. Since I get only one letter on the report card, I use these same letter grades for the purpose of this rubric.

There are four main sections of the rubric I use: volume and variety, thoughtfulness, organization, and frequency. Three of these sections are also in my writer's notebook rubric, and I have these sections the same on purpose. The notebooks are supposed to be similar—using strategies, focusing on thinking, and student ownership. I found it helpful to use this rubric to help kids see the reader's notebook more like a writer's notebook rather than their traditional reading journal they may have had in other years. Also, the consistency helps both students and parents understand how these notebooks are being used—as a tool for thinking more deeply.

The rubric in Figure 6.6 is set for fourth graders based on their general skills in the beginning of the year and can be adjusted depending on the grade level and skill level of the students. I've included the rubric to help demonstrate how it is used to assess notebooks and to think more deeply about the different categories.

Volume and Variety

This section of the rubric looks at how much students write each time, as well as how they approach each entry. For my students, it's reasonable to expect about a page per entry. In general, when students are trying to write four or five pages, they often fall into a retelling of the text they have just read, whereas anything less than a page seems to be enough for a summary

Figure 6.6

Reader's Notebook Rubric

Criteria	A	B	C	D
Volume and Variety	Entries are mostly one page. Student has used a variety of notebook and comprehension strategies.	Entries are about a page long. Student has tried different notebook strategies but tends to use only strategies teacher requests.	Entries vary in length. Student attempts different strategies but tends to use retelling and summary as primary tools.	Entries are within a half of a page. Little attempt is made to try different strategies as talked about in class.
Thoughtfulness	Entries are reflective and may reveal new understandings about the text. Student is careful to use proper GUMS.	Entries are thoughtful and demonstrate use of the different comprehension strategies. Student is careful with GUMS.	Entries show a limited understanding of the text beyond retelling. Student has made several errors with GUMS.	The entry is riddled with errors in GUMS. It demonstrates little thought beyond the story line.
Organization	Entries are organized in a manner that is useful to the reader. Use of paragraphs and a logical order of ideas are apparent.	Entries are somewhat organized. Text is in a logical order and may be arranged in paragraphs.	Entry organization seems haphazard, skipping from one idea to the next. Little explanation supports new ideas.	Ideas in the entry are not organized.
Frequency	At least 90 percent of required entries are completed.	At least 80 percent of required entries are completed.	At least 74 percent of required entries are completed.	73 percent or less of the required entries are completed.

and nothing more. A page, however, seems long enough to get beyond a summary but manageable enough that students won't have to rely on retelling to finish the entry.

For variety, I'm looking to see if students are trying different strategies I've presented in class. Or are they relying on just one or two favorites to get them by? By looking at the ways students approach their entries, I glean insight into their thought processes. Is there a fallback strategy that they use when a book is a bit too difficult? When they read an easier text, do they try more difficult strategies, or are they choosing texts that do not make them think? Do they demonstrate thinking in the different areas of the comprehension strategies? By looking at what the students are doing or not doing in their entries, I know not only if they're in a just-right book, but also if they are engaged in the book that they are reading.

Thoughtfulness

The thoughtfulness category is the least objective on the rubric. Yet I do tell my students and parents the qualities of a thoughtful entry, which consists of the following:

» It looks like the student put some effort into it. It's neat and the GUMS have been edited.

» It goes beyond a summary or retelling. Most of the entries are new thoughts from the student, not repeated ideas from the book.

» It is more interesting than my grocery list. It has voice and is peppered with examples from the text. It does not simply retell the story.

» It demonstrates a deeper understanding than just the story. Students display higher-level thinking skills, such as comparing and contrasting, connecting, inferring, or making predictions, over several events at once.

I model thoughtful entries on a regular basis—especially as I introduce new notebook strategies. I also use student samples to show kids what others their age can do. This is an important step in the process of keeping notebooks. Because there are no right or wrong answers, many students are uncomfortable with the blank page. Giving them examples and modeling the process of reading, thinking, and writing helps students push their own thinking.

Organization

The reader's notebook is different from a writer's notebook in many ways. One key difference is that the reader's notebook is in some ways a record of the inner conversation between a reader and the text. Because readers are responding to more than one event, chapter, or part of the text they're reading and because they may be responding in one entry based on several days of reading, they have time and material to organize.

Although a writer's notebook may have entries that seem like a rambling of thoughts, the reader's notebook shouldn't. Students are reading organized texts before they write. They usually have a strategy they're working on that helps organize their thinking. Plus, by using the text to help develop their ideas, students have time to organize their thoughts before they write. Unlike a writer's notebook, where students are generating at least a page a day, in the reader's notebook, students are writing an entry over several days.

When looking at an organized entry, I expect to see paragraphs. Paragraphs should have topic sentences and supporting details. I'm looking for transition sentences to help move the entry swiftly from one paragraph to another. And the paragraphs should be arranged in a logical order, so that the entry is fluid. This sounds a bit harsh and like it's a lot of work for students. Yet I do believe that children need practice organizing their thoughts in their heads—not only in a prewriting activity. Kids need practice thinking about one idea for more than a sentence. Including criteria like this on the rubric focuses student attention not only on what they're thinking but also on how they're explaining their thinking.

Frequency

For frequency, I'm simply looking for a number. If I collect notebooks every two weeks, and we wrote in them twice a week, I'm looking for four completed entries. I use my lesson-plan book to inform me of the number of strategies I've introduced, the number of entries I requested at school, and any homework assignments I may have given. Then I take a percentage based on our district's grading scale. It's simple, matter of fact, and up front. It's either the easiest way to get an A on the rubric or a sure-fire way to get caught for ignoring the assignments.

Putting It All Together

When I work with teachers, they're usually anxious to get to the assessment part of the day. I understand that. As a teacher, when I'm at a workshop, I want to know how this will fit in my grade book. If I emphasize this process, how do I evaluate it? Many people want to dismiss these concerns, believing that our focus should be on the process rather than the result. In reality, however, we have limited time and students have to earn a grade at the end of each grading period. It's a fact of our life as teachers and an expectation on the part of our communities.

The rubric lightens some of this pressure. Because the rubric is used over several entries, I don't have to collect the notebooks each time the kids write and return them immediately. In addition, I'm not going over every single entry with a fine-tooth comb, nor am I writing back to each student. (I always seem to write more than they did, anyway.) Yet the rubric gives clear expectations and criteria by which those expectations will be evaluated. This gives students—and parents—a sense of structure in my grading process.

In general, I make copies of the rubric, highlight what the students are doing in each category, and do a quick average of the grades for each criteria. Then I put that in my grade book. It's simple, yet effective. I write each child a one- to two-sentence note, and then I move on to the next notebook. This actually takes some discipline on my part. There are notebooks in which I want to write a lot—questions, suggestions, and so forth—but I'm trying to balance my professional life and personal life at the same time. Keeping to this rubric and one or two sentences, I'm able to give feedback to my students without taking up a whole Saturday and, by using an assortment of student self-assessments and teacher assessments, I've found a balance in my classroom too. It's one in which students have clear expectations and gain timely feedback. I find the process to be manageable enough to maintain throughout the school year and informative enough to know my students' strengths and weaknesses. And parents feel informed and empowered to help their children by knowing what is expected and how their child is assessed regularly.

Some teachers like a point system. It makes them feel like the rubric is more objective. That's fine with me. It's important for teachers to adjust the rubric to match their teaching style, curriculum objectives, and any grading requirements they need to adhere to. The important thing is to remain consistent. Consistently use the rubric to assess students. Consistently use points on the rubric or not. An A on the rubric in the fall should be consistent with an A on the rubric in the spring. Likewise, an A for one child's notebook should be consistent with an A on another notebook.

· ※ · ※ · ※ ·

Assessment shouldn't be a bad word; it should play a key role at the intersection of planning and instruction. It should enable us to find out more about our students and their thought processes so that our teaching is informed and we can plan the lessons they need next as they travel back and forth across that bridge between reading and writing.

Final Thoughts

I have several professional books that are well loved: earmarked, highlighted, and worn down. Yet my teaching style doesn't necessarily reflect the authors' exactly. I've given myself room to evolve—starting from what I've read and researched and moving toward an expression of my own understanding of my students, my curriculum, and my teaching ability. That is my hope for readers of this book.

Even as I wrote this book, my understanding and practice evolved from where it was the year prior. It's important to allow ourselves, as teachers, to learn and move forward in our thinking as we work with students. I hope this book gives you a starting place—or a springboard—from which to move your students further in their journey to become better readers. More important, I hope it sparks other ideas in your teaching that help your students read more deeply.

We know that strong writers are strong readers. Reading, in a way, is the writer's research. By developing strategies to help our students think and write about text, we not only help them become better readers, we also define the connection between reading and writing. In this vein, I try to remind myself to remain open to my students' ideas as they see new ways to push their own thinking about reading. New thinking is waiting to be discovered—just as new stories are waiting to be written.

Appendix

Determining Purpose for a Reader's Notebook

Questions to Ask Yourself	My Personal Responses
1. What *reading* curriculum objectives am I trying to accomplish using the reader's notebook as a tool?	
2. What *writing* curriculum objectives will the reader's notebook support?	
3. How often will students write in their reader's notebooks?	
4. What will students be responsible for having in their reader's notebooks?	

Teacher Form: Guiding Questions

Category of Thinking	Questions I Ask Myself and Possible Answers	Possible Guiding Questions for Students
Student as a Reader	What kind of reading behaviors have we talked about lately?	
Comprehension Strategies	What strategies have we been focusing on in mini-lessons?	
Notebook Strategies	Which notebook strategies have I introduced and which ones have the students been practicing?	
Effort	What qualities are the students aware of that demonstrate their effort?	

Student Form: Guiding Questions

Category of Thinking	Guiding Questions for Students
Student as a Reader	How has learning about rising action and climax helped you understand your book(s) better? What is one thing you want to improve about your reading?
Comprehension Strategies	What kind of visualizing do you find yourself doing most? How does this help you understand the story? What gets in your way of "being in" the story?
Notebook Strategies	We have used and practiced four strategies lately. Which one has been the most helpful for your thinking about reading? Which one is still confusing or not helpful to you? Explain to help me understand your opinion.
Effort	As you reread your entries, have you put forth your best effort? Do your entries sound like the thinking in your mind? Have you practiced good writing habits that include attention to punctuation and spelling?

Jennifer Moon's Reading Response Rubric

Rubric for Reading Response	Excellent	Good	Attempting	No Attempt
Capturing Your Thinking I talked about at least three different ideas I had about the book, and I showed my thinking by using some of these strategies: 1. Discussing my thinking about the story (Characters, Setting, Plot, Solution, Theme, etc.) 2. Connecting—showing evidence from the book 3. Predicting/Inferring 4. Questioning 5. Reacting to what is happening in the story I answered the questions my teacher asked me from my last letter in complete sentences.	4	3	2	1
Thoughtfulness/Details I supported my thoughts with evidence from the text. I explained my thinking with telling why I think what I do (because . . .). I showed that I understand my job as a reader and a writer for my response. I put effort into my letter with meaningful thinking and/or questioning about the book I am responding to.	4	3	2	1
Clarity I wrote a response that makes sense. It was easy for the reader to understand my thinking. I showed the ability to express my thinking clearly with complete sentences.	4	3	2	1

Rubric for Reading Response	Excellent	Good	Attempting	No Attempt
Voice/Personality My response is interesting to read, not just a boring list of ideas. It has comments about my thinking (What would I do? How would I feel?).	4	3	2	1
Grammar, Usage, Mechanics, and Spelling (GUMS), Timeliness, and Neatness My response was edited for proper grammar and spelling. It was turned in on time and written neatly. I had all the parts of a letter. I wrote a new paragraph for each new thought/idea.	4	3	2	1

Reader's Notebook Rubric

Criteria	A	B	C	D
Volume and Variety	Entries are mostly one page. Student has used a variety of notebook and comprehension strategies.	Entries are about a page long. Student has tried different notebook strategies but tends to use only strategies teacher requests.	Entries vary in length. Student attempts different strategies but tends to use retelling and summary as primary tools.	Entries are within a half of a page. Little attempt is made to try different strategies as talked about in class.
Thoughtfulness	Entries are reflective and may reveal new understandings about the text. Student is careful to use proper GUMS.	Entries are thoughtful and demonstrate use of the different comprehension strategies. Student is careful with GUMS.	Entries show a limited understanding of the text beyond retelling. Student has made several errors with GUMS.	The entry is riddled with errors in GUMS. It demonstrates little thought beyond the story line.
Organization	Entries are organized in a manner that is useful to the reader. Use of paragraphs and a logical order of ideas are apparent.	Entries are somewhat organized. Text is in a logical order and may be arranged in paragraphs.	Entry organization seems haphazard, skipping from one idea to the next. Little explanation supports new ideas.	Ideas in the entry are not organized.
Frequency	At least 90 percent of required entries are completed.	At least 80 percent of required entries are completed.	At least 74 percent of required entries are completed.	73 percent or less of the required entries are completed.

References

Anderson, Jeff. 2005. *Mechanically Inclined: Building Grammar, Usage, and Style into Writer's Workshop*. Portland, ME: Stenhouse.

Atwell, Nancie. 1987. *In the Middle: Writing, Reading, and Learning with Adolescents*. Portsmouth, NH: Boynton/Cook.

Avi. 2005. *Poppy*. New York: HarperTrophy.

Buckley, Michael. 2007. *The Fairy-Tale Detectives*. New York: Amulet.

Buckner, Aimee. 2005. *Notebook Know-How: Strategies for the Writer's Notebook*. Portland, ME: Stenhouse.

Calkins, Lucy McCormick. 2000. *The Art of Teaching Reading*. Columbus, OH: Allyn & Bacon.

Calkins, Lucy, and Shelley Harwayne. 1990. *Living Between the Lines*. Portsmouth, NH: Heinemann.

Calkins, Lucy, et al. 2007. *Units of Study for Teaching Writing: Grades 3–5*. Portsmouth, NH: Heinemann.

Cary, Alice. 1997. "Gary Paulsen on the Go—Sleds, Motorcycles and Sailboats." BookPage. http://www.bookpage.com/9711bp/firstperson2 .html.

Clements, Andrew. 2006. *The Last Holiday Concert.* New York: Aladdin.

Coville, Bruce. 1992. *Goblins in the Castle.* New York: Simon & Schuster.

Daniels, Harvey. 2002. *Literature Circles: Voice and Choice in the Student Centered Classroom.* 2nd ed. Portland, ME: Stenhouse.

Edwards, Julie Andrews. 1996. *The Last of the Really Great Whangdoodles.* New York: HarperCollins.

Fletcher, Ralph, and JoAnn Portalupi. 2007. *Craft Lessons: Teaching Writing K–8.* Portland, ME: Stenhouse.

Fountas, Irene C., and Gay Su Pinnell. 2001. *Guiding Readers and Writers Grades 3–6: Teaching Comprehension, Genre, and Content Literacy.* Portsmouth, NH: Heinemann.

Freedman, Russell. 1992. *Indian Chiefs.* New York: Holiday House.

Friedrich, Elizabeth. 1999. *Leah's Pony.* Honesdale, PA: Boyds Mills.

Gallagher, Kelly. 2004. *Deeper Reading: Comprehending Challenging Texts, 4–12.* Portland, ME: Stenhouse.

Graves, Donald. 1983. *Writing: Teachers and Children at Work.* Portsmouth, NH: Heinemann.

Harvey, Stephanie. 1998. *Nonfiction Matters: Reading, Writing, and Research in Grades 3–8.* Portland, ME: Stenhouse.

Harvey, Stephanie, and Anne Goudvis. 2005. *The Comprehension Toolkit: Language and Lessons for Active Literacy.* Portsmouth, NH: Heinemann.

———. 2000/2007. *Strategies That Work: Teaching Comprehension for Understanding and Engagement.* 2nd ed. Portland, ME: Stenhouse.

Henkes, Kevin. 1996. *Chrysanthemum.* New York: HarperTrophy.

———. 2004. *Lilly's Purple Plastic Purse.* New York: Scholastic.

Hughes, Langston. 1994. "Dreams." In *The Dream Keeper and Other Poems.* New York: Scholastic.

King, Stephen. 2000. *On Writing: A Memoir of the Craft.* New York: Scribner.

Kramer, Stephen. 1992. *Lightning.* Minneapolis, MN: Carolrhoda Books.

———. 1995. *Caves.* Minneapolis, MN: Carolrhoda Books.

Krull, Kathleen. 2003. *Harvesting Hope: The Story of Cesar Chavez.* New York: Harcourt Children's Books.

———. 2005. *Houdini: World's Greatest Mystery Man and Escape King.* New York: Walker Books for Young Readers.

Lent, Releah Cossett. 2006. *Engaging Adolescent Learners: A Guide for Content-Area Teachers.* Portsmouth, NH: Heinemann.

Lester, Julius. 1994. *John Henry.* New York: Dial.

Levine, Ellen. 2007. *Henry's Freedom Box: A True Story from the Underground Railroad.* New York: Scholastic.

Moss, Miriam. 2005. *This Is the Tree: A Story of the Baobab.* La Jolla, CA: Kane/Miller.

Paulsen, Gary. 1994. *Mr. Tucket.* New York: Delacorte.

Pearson, P. D., and M. C. Gallagher. 1983. "The Instruction of Reading Comprehension." *Contemporary Educational Psychology* 8: 317–344.

Portalupi, JoAnn, and Ralph Fletcher. 2004. *Teaching the Qualities of Writing.* Portsmouth, NH: Heinemann.

Ray, Katie Wood. 1999. *Wondrous Words: Writers and Writing in the Elementary Classroom.* Urbana, IL: NCTE.

———. 2006. *Study Driven: A Framework for Planning Units of Study in the Writing Workshop.* Portsmouth, NH: Heinemann.

Rosenblatt, Louise. 2005. *Making Meaning with Texts.* Portsmouth, NH: Heinemann.

Rowling, J. K. 1998. *Harry Potter and the Sorcerer's Stone.* New York: Scholastic.

Ruckman, Ivy. 1986. *Night of the Twisters.* New York: HarperTrophy.

Rushton, Stephen P., Janice Eitelgeorge, and Ruby Zickafoose. 2003. "Connecting Brian Cambourne's Conditions of Learning Theory to Brain/Mind Principles: Implications for Early Childhood Educators." *Early Childhood Education Journal* 31 (1):11–21.

Rylant, Cynthia. 1998. *Every Living Thing.* New York: Aladdin.

Sachar, Louis. 2000. *Holes.* New York: Scholastic.

Senisi, Ellen. 1999. *Reading Grows.* Morton Grove, IL: Albert Whitman.

Sibberson, Franki, and Karen Szymusiak. 2003. *Still Learning to Read: Teaching Students in Grades 3–6.* Portland, ME: Stenhouse.

Smith, Frank. 1988. *Joining the Literacy Club: Further Essays into Education.* Portsmouth, NH: Heinemann.

Spinelli, Jerry. 1990. *Maniac Magee.* Boston: Little, Brown.

Szymusiak, Karen, and Franki Sibberson. 2001. *Beyond Leveled Books: Supporting Transitional Readers in Grades 2–5.* Portland, ME: Stenhouse.

Tovani, Cris. 2000. *I Read It, but I Don't Get It.* Portland, ME: Stenhouse.

Van de Walle, John A., and LouAnn H. Lovin. 2005. *Teaching Student-Centered Mathematics Grades K–3.* Columbus, OH: Allyn & Bacon.

Vygotsky, Lev. S. 1978. *Mind in Society: The Development of Higher Psychological Processes.* Cambridge, MA: Harvard University Press.

White, E. B. 1974. *Charlotte's Web.* New York: HarperTrophy.